Methods for Teaching Medicine

Teaching Medicine Series

Jack Ende, MD, MACP
Series Editor

Methods for Teaching Medicine

Kelley M. Skeff, MD, PhD, MACP
Georgette A. Stratos, PhD
Editors

ACP Press
American College of Physicians • Philadelphia, Pennsylvania

Director, Publishing Operations: Linda Drumheller
Developmental Editor: Marla Sussman
Production Editor: Suzanne Meyers
Publishing Coordinator: Angela Gabella
Cover Design: Kate Nichols
Index: Kathleen Patterson

Printed in the United States of America
Printing/Binding by Versa Press
Composition by ACP Graphic Services

Library of Congress Cataloging-in-Publication Data

Methods for teaching medicine / [edited by] Kelley Skeff and Georgette Stratos.
     p. ; cm. -- (ACP teaching medicine series)
   Includes bibliographical references and index.
   ISBN 978-1-934465-42-4
   1. Medicine--Study and teaching. I. Skeff, Kelley II. Stratos, Georgette III.
American College of Physicians. IV. Series: ACP teaching medicine series.
   [DNLM: 1. Education, Medical--methods. 2. Teaching--methods.
W 18 M592 2010]
   R735.M48 2010
   610.76--dc22
                                        2009053099

10 11 12 13 14 / 10 9 8 7 6 5 4 3 2 1

Contributors

David Davis, MD, CCFP, FCFP, RCPS(C)(Hon)
Adjunct Professor
Faculty of Medicine
University of Toronto
Toronto, Canada
Senior Director
Association of American Medical Colleges
Washington, DC

Jack Ende, MD, MACP
Professor of Medicine
University of Pennsylvania School of Medicine
Philadelphia, Pennsylvania
Chief, Department of Medicine
Penn Presbyterian Medical Center
Philadelphia, Pennsylvania

Robert D. Fox, EdD
Professor Emeritus of Educational Leadership and Policy Studies
University of Oklahoma
Norman, Oklahoma

David E. Kern, MD, MPH
Professor of Medicine
Johns Hopkins University School of Medicine
Director, Division of General Internal Medicine
Johns Hopkins Bayview Medical Center
Baltimore, Maryland

Scott C. Litin, MD, MACP
Professor of Medicine
Mayo Clinic College of Medicine
Rochester, Minnesota

Karen Mann, PhD
Professor, Division of Medical Education
Faculty of Medicine
Dalhousie University
Halifax, Nova Scotia, Canada

Paul O'Neill, MBChB, MD, FRCP (London)
Professor of Medical Education
Manchester Medical School
University of Manchester
Manchester, United Kingdom

Kelley M. Skeff, MD, PhD, MACP
Professor of Medicine
Department of Internal Medicine
Vice-Chair for Education
Department of Medicine
Stanford University School of Medicine
Palo Alto, California

Yvonne Steinert, PhD
Director, Centre for Medical Education
Associate Dean, Faculty Development
Faculty of Medicine
McGill University
Montreal, Quebec, Canada

Georgette A. Stratos, PhD
Senior Research Scholar
Stanford University School of Medicine
Stanford, California

Patricia A. Thomas, MD, FACP
Associate Professor of Medicine
Associate Dean for Curriculum
Johns Hopkins University School of Medicine
Baltimore, Maryland

This book is dedicated to the 319 medical faculty who have attended our various facilitator-training programs at the Stanford Faculty Development Center with the goal of improving their own teaching and helping their colleagues to do the same. These faculty have come from institutions affiliated with over 65% of U.S. medical schools and from 15 countries outside the United States. To us, they epitomize the large number of medical faculty who care deeply about their role as teachers and who wish to do the very best for the trainees and their patients.

Acknowledgments

We have been fortunate to have known and been influenced by two major contributors to the field of education, Lee Shulman and the late Nathan Gage. They represent an entire group of investigators and thinkers who have advanced the field of education inside and outside of medicine. We gratefully acknowledge their important contributions to our work and, therefore, to this book.

Contents

Visit www.acponline.org/acp_press/teaching
for additional information.

About the *Teaching Medicine* Series

This book series, *Teaching Medicine*, represents a major initiative from the American College of Physicians. It is intended for College members but also for the profession as a whole. Internists, family physicians, subspecialists, surgical colleagues, nurse practitioners, and physician assistants—indeed, anyone involved with medical education—should find this book series useful as they pursue one of the greatest privileges of the profession: the opportunity to teach and make a difference in the lives of learners and their patients. The series is composed of six books:

- *Theory and Practice of Teaching Medicine*, edited by me, considers how medical learners learn (how to be doctors), how medical teachers teach, and how they (the teachers) might learn to teach better.

- *Methods for Teaching Medicine*, edited by Kelley M. Skeff and Georgette A. Stratos, builds on this foundation but focuses on the actual methods that medical teachers use. This book explores the full range of techniques that encourage learning within groups. The authors present a conceptual framework and guiding perspectives for understanding teaching; the factors that support choices for particular teaching methods (such as lecturing vs. small group discussion); and practical advice for preceptors, attendings, lecturers, discussion leaders, workshop leaders, and, finally, course directors charged with running programs for continuing medical education.

- *Teaching in Your Office*, edited by Patrick C. Alguire, Dawn E. DeWitt, Linda E. Pinsky, and Gary S. Ferenchick, will be familiar to many teaching internists. It has been reissued as part of this series. This book remains the office-based preceptor's single most useful resource for preparing to receive medical students and residents into an ambulatory practice setting or, among those already engaged in office-based teaching, for learning how to do it even better.

- *Teaching in the Hospital* is edited by Jeff Wiese and considers the challenges and rewards of teaching in that particular setting. Hospitalists as well as more traditional internists who attend on the inpatient service will be interested in the insightful advice that this book provides. This advice focuses not only on how to conduct rounds and encourage learning among students and house officers but also on how to frame and orient the content of rounds for some of the more frequently encountered inpatient conditions.

- *Mentoring in Academic Medicine,* edited by Holly J. Humphrey, considers professional development across the continuum of medical education, from issues pertaining to students to residents to faculty themselves, as well as issues pertaining to professional development of special populations. Here is where the important contributions of mentors and role models are explored in detail.

- *Leadership Careers in Medical Education* concludes this series. Edited by Louis Pangaro, this book is written for members of the medical faculty who are pursuing—or who are considering—careers as clerkship directors, residency program directors, or educational leaders of departments or medical schools, careers that require not only leadership skill but also a deep understanding of the organization and administration of internal medicine's educational enterprise. This book explores the theory and practice of educational leadership, including curricular design and evaluation; and offers insightful profiles of many of internal medicine's most prominent leaders.

Jack Ende, MD, MACP
Philadelphia, 2010

Introduction: Tools to Improve Your Effectiveness as a Teacher

Teachers of internal medicine are typically motivated by the ultimate goal of improving the patient care provided by their students and house staff. Through their teaching role, they have a powerful impact on future generations of physicians and patients. They are also driven by the enjoyment of teaching the exciting and the ever-changing science of internal medicine, as well as the patient-centered care so needed in today's world. Being a teacher of internal medicine can be a gratifying role. At the same time, it can be quite difficult. It requires teaching complex content that covers the entire spectrum of disease and the psychosocial aspects facing a variety of patients; teaching across the levels of learners from students to colleagues; and teaching in a wide variety of settings from the bedside to the lecture hall, from the clinic to the wards, from the community to the university. This book is written to help these teachers meet the challenge of this important professional role.

What made us excited to contribute to this book? We have had the good fortune in our faculty development programs to work with many clinical teachers—predominantly from internal medicine—over the past 3 decades. We have been consistently impressed with the dedication of these teachers, who demonstrate unswerving commitment to both their trainees and the future of the field of medicine. In addition, we have seen these teachers benefit from effective methods to improve teaching. In particular, we have first-hand experience seeing teachers benefit from mastering the types of tools described in this book. These benefits range from increased enthusiasm for teaching to more informed decision-making about instructional options to helping learners attain their personal and professional goals.

We believe you will find this a helpful book. It contains a set of practical tools for improving your teaching across a broad spectrum of instructional methods. The focus is primarily on methods affecting groups of learners, small and large. The book offers teaching aids at two levels: conceptual frameworks and concrete "how-to" tips. The former can enhance the ways you think about teaching, and the latter will provide specific suggestions for changing your teaching methods. The book is designed to help you improve your teaching effectiveness by assisting you in analyzing your teaching using educational principles, discriminating and choosing between teaching methods to accomplish your educational goals, and identifying and implementing practical techniques for improving teaching.

In chapter 1, "Developing Expertise in Teaching," we pass on a set of guiding perspectives gleaned from the field of education and from personal experience that we feel are critical to the successful design and delivery of faculty development programs for medical teachers. We also present an educational framework that teachers can use as a conceptual tool for analyzing teaching across different content areas, types of learners, and educational contexts. In chapter 2, "From Curricular Goals to Instruction: Choosing Methods of Instruction," Patricia A. Thomas, MD, and David E. Kern, MD, review principles for developing effective curricular goals, describe the array of instructional methods typically used to teach medicine, and offer helpful suggestions for deciding which methods to use on the basis of one's educational goals.

Chapters 3 through 6 are devoted to more in-depth discussions of recommended teaching techniques associated with four methods regularly used in internal medicine training: lectures, small-group discussions, workshops, and continuing medical education. In chapter 3, "The Lecture: Tips to Make Your Next Presentations Go Better Than Your Last," Scott C. Litin, MD, and Jack Ende, MD, draw on their extensive experience in offering a spirited series of recommendations for enhancing presentations to large groups. The authors of chapter 4, Karen Mann, PhD, and Paul O'Neill, MD, present several teaching scenarios to guide teachers in "Facilitating a Small Group Discussion." They encourage the reader to analyze these scenarios by applying key educational principles (such as active learning, collaborative learning, critical reflection, and knowledge transfer). Yvonne Steinert, PhD, offers an accessible and highly practical set of guidelines in chapter 5, "How to Design and Conduct Effective Workshops." She provides "how-to" tips for a range of common instructional strategies used in workshops (for example, buzz groups, case vignettes, role plays, standardized patients, and debates). In the final chapter, "Helping Physicians Learn and Change Their Practice Performance: Principles for Effective Continuing Medical Education," David Davis, MD, and Robert D. Fox, EdD, identify innovative, new directions for developing and delivering successful continuing education of practicing physicians. The authors contemplate the implications and reality for moving from the traditional CME (continuing medical education) model to a new CPD (continuing professional development) paradigm.

We hope this book promotes the kind of reflection that facilitates your analysis of your own teaching, and informs your choices of teaching methods and behaviors. Given the inherent variability in the effectiveness of any teaching method with different groups of learners, we encourage you to try new or different approaches to teaching as experimentalists, evaluating their effectiveness with your particular group of learners. Your importance as a teacher of internal medicine in the forthcoming era cannot be overemphasized. We hope that this book enhances your gratification in that role.

Kelley M. Skeff, MD, PhD, MACP
Georgette A. Stratos, PhD
Stanford, California, 2010

1

Developing Expertise in Teaching

Kelley M. Skeff, MD, PhD, MACP
Georgette A. Stratos, PhD

A s teachers prepare to teach, as well as make on-the-spot decisions regarding approaches and specific behaviors to use in their
teaching, they may be influenced by many factors, including
belief systems, habits, experience, intuition, and goals for their learners. This chapter first identifies guiding perspectives that sharpen our
view of expertise in teaching; an organizing framework for analyzing
teaching is then described. This systematic framework for analyzing
teaching that has evolved over the 3 decades of the authors' work at the
Stanford Faculty Development Center for Medical Teachers. This overarching structure applies across a variety of teaching methods. Thus,
the hope is that these guiding perspectives and framework enable you
to better understand, select, and implement the recommendations
made in later chapters.

❖ Guiding Perspectives for Development as a Teaching Professional

Research on teaching has guided the design and conduct teaching
improvement programs and the training of others as faculty developers. Five perspectives distilled from this research are particularly helpful in elucidating the factors involved in the professional development
of teachers (Box 1-1). In becoming familiar with these perspectives,

KEY POINTS

- The development of teaching expertise can be facilitated by consideration of key guiding principles.
- Experience leads to expertise. With increased expertise in a given teaching setting or content, teachers may implement techniques that they have found effective, stepping back to reexamine the teaching methods when learners do not appear to be successful in mastering the content. Through this process they move along the spectrum from novice to expert.
- Pedagogical principles intersect with the content being taught (pedagogical content knowledge). The most effective teachers are those with special knowledge of the conceptual organization and analogies regarding their content that enable learners at different levels to master the content area.
- Reflection on one's teaching approaches fosters continuing improvement. Professionals can apply their knowledge base and experience to improving their performance the next time the situation is encountered.
- Both scientific and artistic bases for teaching provide valuable guidance to teachers. Although teachers can be guided by a scientific basis, they can rely on individual artistry in departing from what is implied by rules, formulas, and algorithms.
- Versatility in teaching approaches can enhance effectiveness. Medical teachers, therefore, should consider expanding their repertoires of specific teaching behaviors and ways they think about teaching.
- A comprehensive, educational framework can be used as a conceptual tool to analyze and improve teaching.

you may better understand aspects of your own teaching that will help you continue toward your goal of teaching excellence.

Guiding Perspective 1: Mastery of the Teaching Craft Is Enabled by Both Experience Itself and Knowledge Gained Through That Experience
David Berliner's research on the development of teaching expertise highlights the importance of experience, and the knowledge and principles

---

Box 1-1. Five Guiding Perspectives on Development as a Teaching Professional

1. Mastery of the teaching craft is enabled by both experience itself and knowledge gained through that experience.
2. Expertise in teaching occurs at the intersection of the knowledge of pedagogy and the knowledge of the content being taught (pedagogical content knowledge).
3. Master teachers use reflection for ongoing improvement.
4. Teaching can be guided by both science and artistry.
5. Teaching effectiveness benefits from versatility.

---

gained from experience (1). Building on the work of Dreyfus and colleagues (2), Berliner described the qualities gained in moving from being a novice to an expert, passing through the phases of advanced beginner, competent teacher, proficient teacher, and finally expert teacher. Box 1-2 summarizes the characteristics of each stage.

As teachers acquire experience and abilities, their processing of the many variables influencing teaching changes from a simplistic, rule-based approach to the automatic processing of the expert. Berliner's work indicates that novices struggle to make sense of complex teaching situations,

---

Box 1-2. From Novice to Expert

Novice: Learns context-free rules to guide behavior

Advanced beginner: Has benefits of experience; recognizes similarities across contexts; builds up episodic knowledge

Competent: Makes conscious choices about priorities and plans; while enacting skills, can judge what is and what is not important as learned through experience

Proficient: Uses a higher level of categorization of experiences to make decisions; incorporates intuition and "know-how"; develops intuition through experience but is still analytic and deliberative in deciding what to do

Expert: Works intuitively, automatically; moves to analysis when things don't go well

---

whereas experts can process detailed information about the learners, content, and setting that enables them to analyze the teaching situation. This work also suggests that stages of expertise may be highly contextualized—a given teacher could be at different stages in different situations. Thus, clinical teachers may be at any of these stages according to their knowledge of teaching or their experience in a given setting or content area. For example, a clinical teacher faced with teaching a new content area or a new group of learners may rely on his or her knowledge of "rules" of effective teaching. With increased expertise in a given teaching setting or content, that teacher may implement techniques that she or he has found effective, only stepping back to reexamine the teaching methods when learners do not appear to be successful in mastering the content; through this process they move along the spectrum from novice to expert.

Berliner also identified a group of teachers he called "postulants," represented by those who had worked in industry, for example, as engineers or scientists, but who were not interested in completing a regular teacher education program. These teachers, observed as part of a research study, were described as being even less familiar with the complexities of the classroom than other professional teachers. Many clinical teachers could be classified as postulant teachers, given that their assignment to and choice of the teaching role may be largely due to their content expertise. Thus, for many medical teachers who fit this description, formal analysis of their teaching may be helpful for gaining a better understanding of the educational variables influencing their teaching.

How can we as teachers speed up the acquisition of the skills and knowledge to move us progressively through the stages of expertise without relying primarily on experience? Berliner's work suggests that teachers advance from novice to expert levels of expertise by learning how to identify "instances of concepts." That is, as novices learn to classify and categorize important experiences that occur during teaching, they can more effectively interpret new episodes and events of teaching. For example, a novice teacher may interpret a trainee's intense questioning as disruptive, possibly even meant to interrupt the teacher's agenda. However, through multiple experiences with many trainees, a more expert teacher can amass a large quantity of knowledge about trainees' behavior. This knowledge provides the basis for making different inferences from the trainees' actions. The experienced teacher will have encountered learners who exhibited the very same action—question asking—but whose intentions were not disruptive; in fact, they were actions intended to satisfy inquisitiveness in a topic.

Thus, the expert teacher may recognize the learner's input as a representation of his or her own personal educational motives and goals, providing an opportunity for the teacher to share the process of defining educational goals with the learner, accepting the learner's input as an opportunity for further education rather than a disruption. In this manner, teachers can relate the examples they face in teaching to principles and concepts that can guide their decision-making for teaching. By providing a conceptual scaffold of categories for interpreting teaching events in this chapter, it is hoped that readers will more efficiently acquire teaching expertise that informs their choices of effective teaching methods.

Guiding Perspective 2: Expertise in Teaching Occurs at the Intersection of the Knowledge of Pedagogy and the Knowledge of the Content Being Taught

Among Lee Shulman's many contributions to the field of education is his introduction of the idea of pedagogical content knowledge (3). Shulman proposed that true expertise in teaching occurs at the intersection of the knowledge of pedagogy and the knowledge of the content being taught (that is, how the content is transformed for the purpose of teaching and learning). Shulman distinguishes this pedagogical content knowledge from that held by a content area expert and from the general pedagogical knowledge that might be shared by teachers from different disciplines. Pedagogical content knowledge is concerned with the representation and formulation of concepts relevant to the content area being taught, such as knowledge of what makes concepts difficult or easy to learn and knowledge of what students bring to the learning situation in regard to the content (for example, their prior knowledge, difficulties, and misconceptions about a particular domain, and potential misapplications of prior knowledge). Pedagogical content knowledge contains "the most regularly taught topics in one's subject area, the most useful forms of representation of those ideas, the most powerful analogies, illustrations, examples, explanations, and demonstrations—in a word, the ways of representing and formulating the subject that make it comprehensible to others" (4).

In the context of teaching internal medicine, the concept of pedagogical content knowledge would imply that the most effective teachers are those with special knowledge of the conceptual organization and analogies regarding their content that enables learners at different levels to master the content area—that is, the content is organized and taught in particularly effective ways for the learners. Master teachers in every field have developed particular approaches to the teaching of their content that make their material more understandable. Shulman's work is particularly relevant to teaching in a field such as internal medicine, with its variety of challenging content, ranging from basic science subjects to issues in health care delivery, from science to the practice of medicine. Expert teachers of internal medicine may develop a variety of pedagogical devices to improve the learner's acquisition of complex topics.

Faced with teaching about acid-base disturbances, renal tubular acidosis, or hypercholesterolemia, an effective teacher of internal medicine could develop a set of explanations, principles, metaphors, schematics, or analogies that can enable learners to meaningfully understand the material, given their current understanding. For example, an explanation of acid-base disturbances may be better understood if the concepts of primary and secondary disorders are used, renal tubular acidosis may be more fully understood in terms of the anatomic location of the defect in the tubule, and explanations of hypercholesterolemia may benefit from a pictorial representation of cholesterol metabolism.

In summary, incorporating pedagogical content knowledge into clinical teaching depends not only on knowledge of the subject but also on greater in-depth knowledge of the types of challenges that learners have in mastering the subject. Thus, the teacher who has not only clinical content but also pedagogical content knowledge has observed a large variety of learners struggle with the content, and is prompted to develop a broader variety of teaching approaches that will enable most learners to master the content. The teaching scripts in section II of *Teaching in the Hospital*, another book in the *Teaching Medicine* series (5), illustrate how this can be implemented in, for example, the inpatient setting; however, the concept is as valid for teaching in the office.

Guiding Perspective 3: Master Teachers Use Reflection for Ongoing Improvement

John Dewey and Donald Schön have made major contributions to the understanding of the utility of thoughtful analysis of one's professional actions. Dewey's concept of "reflective thought" highlights the phases occurring when one attempts to understand an event or problem that includes uncertainty (6). For example, when faced with a complex teaching situation, such as a difficult or challenging learner, where the most effective teaching behavior is not obvious, professional reflection is necessary to consider and make judgments about teaching approaches. Dewey explained that one defines the challenge, reasons inductively to identify possible solutions, elaborates ideas, and then tests hypotheses through overt or imaginative action.

A half-century later, Schön (7) elaborated a similar process in which people move from concrete experiences to critical reflection to the identification of new perspectives as they incorporate new approaches in their professional role. Schön pointed out the importance of the reflection process to all professionals, coining the terms "reflection-on-action" as well as "reflection-in-action."

Reflection-on-action refers to the important activity of all professionals to think back and "reflect on" whatever professional behavior they have exhibited. With this reflection, professionals can apply their knowledge base and experience to improving their performance the next time the situation is encountered. Although this important formal and deliberate activity is a part of all professionals' lives, it may be done less by expert professionals when they are dealing with their everyday professional life. Such experts often move to an essentially automatic process that incorporates and uses what they have learned to be important, with less attention to phenomena that do not fit with what they have learned. This process is called *reflection-in-action*. Thus, they have learned in their acquisition of expertise to selectively neglect distracting issues that have not been as important given their experience. Clinical teachers may use both reflection-on-action and reflection-in-action on the basis of their experience and level of expertise.

Certain practices can enhance the effectiveness of self-reflection in bringing about new ideas or new understandings, such as obtaining the perspectives of others, especially those with different backgrounds and perspectives, and using preestablished criteria or a framework (see Table 1-1) to increase understanding. Our faculty development programs have emphasized the latter approach. This approach to using a framework can be labeled "reflection-*about*-action." Having a framework for a systematic review provides a teacher with a method for periodic and ongoing reflection *about* the entire process of teaching. Using a framework for reflection-about-action embodies a process that can be used by novices and experts alike to identify areas for ongoing professional growth or understanding.

Guiding Perspective 4: Teaching Can Be Guided by Both Science and Artistry

Nathaniel Gage, a pioneer in research on teaching, wrote about the value of a scientific basis for the art of teaching (8). He suggested that practical enterprises such as teaching, or medicine, or engineering have both scientific and artistic components. A scientific basis consists of "knowledge of regular, nonchance relationships in the realm of events with which the practice is concerned. The relationships need not be perfect or even close to perfect. Rather, the relationships need merely be better than those that would occur by chance" (8). A scientific basis presents variables that have been identified and related to other variables by scientific methods. These variables related to teaching, such as clarity of explanation, demonstration of enthusiasm, and the interactions of these with other variables, can provide a teacher with guidance for changing teaching.

However, Gage also argues that because teaching so often involves a highly complex interaction of variables, the application of the scientific basis by a teacher in real-world practice will always require artistry. That is, the teacher relies on artistry in making choices about teaching behaviors or strategies, using judgment, intuition, creativity, improvisation, and insight to handle the unpredicted, and depart from rules, formulas, and algorithms (8).

For example, Gage refers to studies indicating that the relationship of teacher criticism and student achievement varies with the academic nature of the student. Criticism can have a less positive effect on the least academic students and a more positive effect on the more academic students. Teachers who are aware of this research finding must then use artistic judgment in deciding how and when to apply it to a group of learners, taking into account, for example, not only the academic nature of the student but also variables such as the emotional state of the learner and the relationship of the teacher with the learner (see also chapter 3 of *Theory and Practice of Teaching Medicine*, also part of the *Teaching Medicine* series [9]). Thus, the teacher must use artistic judgment about variables not guided by science. Again, this process is familiar to clinicians who weigh many aspects about patients that may not be addressed by the scientific literature.

The suggestions for teaching internal medicine that are offered in this book are grounded, whenever possible, in educational theory and research. However, when these recommendations are put into practice, it is critical to recognize that although teachers can be guided by a scientific basis, they can rely on individual artistry in departing from what is implied by rules, formulas, and algorithms. Thus, an individual's judgment in any given teaching interaction can be influenced by intuition, creativity, improvisation, and their knowledge of that particular situation, including knowledge of the student, the context, and their own abilities.

Guiding Perspective 5: Teaching Effectiveness Benefits From Versatility
The four perspectives described above emphasize the complexity of the variables that can lead to teaching excellence: the importance of experience, the integration of the content of teaching with pedagogy, the role of ongoing professional reflection, and the resultant application of both teaching principles as science and professional judgment as art. It is unwise to suggest there is a science of teaching that implies "good" teaching can be achieved by adherence to a set of rigorous laws that yield high predictability and control. With respect to the complexity that characterizes clinical teaching in particular, a prescriptive approach to teaching improvement that proposes only rules for being an effective teacher has a low probability of being

successful over time. Clinical teachers face countless variations in content, learners, and contexts. Therefore, to enhance the ongoing effectiveness that encompasses these variables, medical teachers should expand their repertoires of specific teaching behaviors and ways they think about teaching. Taking this perspective, teachers become teaching experimentalists, considering new approaches to conceptualizing teaching as well as selecting and implementing a variety of teaching behaviors, and then examining subsequent learning outcomes. In essence, versatility can be considered the core characteristic of ongoing teaching effectiveness.

Faculty can hold too tightly to a given set of behaviors or a particular teaching philosophy and, thus, be impeded from identifying and implementing new effective teaching behaviors. In addition, teachers should avoid the belief that there is a "best" way of teaching. Thus, we recommend an open philosophy, suggesting that a more extensive repertoire of teaching behaviors and approaches will hold greater promise in helping teachers accommodate to the complex situations they face. It is in this spirit that a variety of tips and suggestions are offered in the chapters that follow. Recognizing that clinical teaching is inherently situation-dependent, the authors of these chapters present a variety of suggestions to help you respond with versatility and artistry as teachers.

❖ An Educational Framework for Analyzing Teaching

This book aims to help teachers enhance their versatility by offering a systematic approach for reflecting on the teaching process and specific recommendations for improving effectiveness when particular instructional methods are used. The next section presents an educational framework for analyzing teaching developed at the Stanford Faculty Development Center for Medical Teachers (Table 1-1).

This framework is being presented early in this book because the educational principles underlying the framework apply to all teaching methods, including those discussed in this book, such as lecturing, discussion groups, workshops, and continuing medical education. Thus, the reader will be able to use this framework to better analyze, interpret, and apply the recommendations made in the chapters covering the various teaching methods.

The act of using a framework to analyze complex systems is familiar to all physicians as they investigate a patient's history using the "review of systems." This framework provides the physician with a safety net or checklist approach that ensures coverage of important areas affecting the patient's health. Similarly, the educational framework offered here is, in a sense, a review of systems for teaching. It provides a systematic way for a

Table 1-1. Categories of the Educational Framework: Formal and Informal Definitions

Category	Formal Definition	Informal Definition
Learning climate	The tone or atmosphere of the teaching setting, including whether it is stimulating and whether learners can comfortably identify and address their limitations	Do the learners want to be there?
Control of session	The manner in which the teaching interaction is focused and paced, as influenced by the teacher's leadership style	Is the session organized and efficient? Is the leadership effective for the educational goals?
Communication of goals	The establishment and explicit expression of a teacher's and/or learners' expectations for the learners	Why are the learners here?
Promotion of understanding and retention	The approaches a teacher can use to 1) explain the content being taught and 2) have the learner meaningfully interact with that content, thus assisting the learner to understand and retain it	What teaching approaches did the teacher use to facilitate learning?
Evaluation of the learners	The process by which the teacher assesses the learners' knowledge, skills, and attitudes, based on educational goals	Are the learners mastering the desired goals?
Feedback to the learners	The process by which the teacher provides learners with information about their performance for the purpose of improving their performance	Do the learners know what the teacher thinks about their performance?
Promotion of self-directed learning	Self-directed learning is the form of learning initiated by the individual learner's needs, goals, and interests; this category deals with approaches the teacher can use to influence motivation and use of resources, thereby fostering self-directed learning	Is learning driven by the learner's motivation?

teacher to reflect on different aspects or categories of teaching and an organized approach for reflecting on past, current, and planned behavior. Space does not permit us to completely describe the educational framework that the authors teach in their course. However, a general description of the framework will provide a systematic structure for considering the many excellent suggestions made in the subsequent chapters of this book and guide ongoing reflections on your own teaching.

This systematic, seven-category framework for analyzing teaching is based on educational theory, empirical studies, and observation of medical teaching interactions (10, 11). The framework has been widely disseminated to clinical and basic science teachers worldwide, through a train-the-trainer faculty development program (12). It has been shown to be useful to teachers who work in different cultures (from Asia to the Middle East) and who hold different teaching responsibilities (from one-on-one PhD mentorship to large-group lecturing). Table 1-1 presents the categories in the framework, with formal and informal definitions. The categories encompass aspects of teaching that are constantly present throughout a teaching session (for example, learning climate and control of session) as well as those that are more episodic (for example, communicating goals, using techniques to promote understanding, evaluating the learners, providing feedback, and fostering the self-directed learning of each individual in the learning team).

This framework offers teachers a conceptual tool that can be used in multiple contexts, when teachers are reflecting on past teaching/learning interactions, planning for future sessions, and analyzing teaching as it unfolds. It can be applied to the analysis of others' teaching as well as to one's own, and has utility across teaching settings. Although the separation of these seven categories is useful for analyzing a teaching interaction, it is important to recognize that this artificial separation is an oversimplification of a highly complex set of interactions between and among the categories. If changes are made in one category, others are affected. If, for example, the learning climate is improved by a teacher showing enthusiasm for the learners, then learners may be more receptive to receiving corrective feedback. Moreover, if the teacher has provided constructive feedback effectively, the learners may feel more comfortable being evaluated by the teacher. In fact, reflection on the interactions between categories can be a useful exercise to illuminate the synergistic and interdependent relationships between these various aspects of teaching.

❖ Applying the Educational Framework to Various Teaching Methods

A general presentation of these categories does not do justice to the complexity of the process of teaching. At the definition level, these categories provide an overall structure for examining the teaching process conceptually, but do not deal with the specific behaviors of teaching. For example, although this chapter identifies "evaluation" of the learners as an important category, it does not discuss specific questioning approaches for evaluating a learner (see chapter 6 in *Teaching in the Hospital* [5]). Nonetheless, having an overall structure for one's analysis can be useful in identifying broad areas for reflection, including the identification of general areas of teaching success and areas for improvement. Physicians recognize this utility of considering broad areas in diagnosis as they consider medical cases. When a physician considers that a particular finding is related to one organ system, a complete review of other organ systems can be illuminating. For example, in diagnosing pulmonary infiltrates, consideration of the complete review of systems may reveal previously unrecognized renal dysfunction, thus leading to a more accurate pulmonary-renal diagnosis, such as Goodpasture syndrome. Similarly, when one is having difficulty with giving feedback while teaching, a consideration of other educational categories may reveal that a confrontational or disrespectful learning climate may be making it difficult for the teacher to provide effective feedback, or that a lack of agreement on educational goals for the learner may be playing a major role in making the feedback less effective.

Thus, the framework can function as a self-assessment checklist for evaluating your own teaching. Considering each definition, you can rate yourself as to whether that category is generally a strong point in your teaching or whether it is an area you wish to improve. It can also function as a powerful conceptual tool for considering approaches to use prospectively (preparing for teaching), in the moment, and retrospectively (reflecting about your teaching) (see also chapter 4 in *Theory and Practice of Teaching Medicine* [9]).

For example, you can turn to the framework after your instincts tell you that a teaching interaction did not go well. By reflecting on the categories, it might be possible to identify an area that could have enhanced your teaching, and to consciously choose a course of action for future interactions. You can also consider the framework in the act of teaching to assess the effectiveness of your teaching and consider alternative approaches.

As you read the rest of this book, try to make an explicit effort to integrate this educational framework with the material presented in each chapter. Each category in the framework applies across the teaching methods presented. For example, whether a teacher is giving a lecture, conducting clinical rounds, or conducting a CME course, it is relevant to consider whether the learning climate of the educational experience is both stimulating and safe enough for learners to "want to be there"; whether the relevance of the goals is recognized by the learners; whether information about the learner's performance is being gathered; whether the learner is informed of this assessment through feedback; or whether the educational experience fosters ongoing, self-directed learning by the participants.

In a book filled with suggestions for thinking about and improving teaching, it's important to acknowledge the difficulty each of us faces when trying to change behaviors that have become part of our automatic repertoire. Many factors can impede our ability to change, including habits and the challenging contexts of teaching. Just recognizing that there are areas we wish to improve may not, in itself, bring about change. However, the hope is that having a set of tools, both conceptual and behavioral, may help each of us overcome barriers that hinder our ability to change and improve our effectiveness. The authors of the following chapters have provided many recommendations for enhancing your teaching effectiveness. By reflecting on these teaching suggestions and considering how they relate to the educational framework presented, you will be able to choose and implement an enhanced variety of teaching behaviors that will make you a more effective teacher in the field of medicine.

REFERENCES

1. **Berliner DC.** The Development of Expertise in Pedagogy. New Orleans, LA: American Association of Colleges for Teacher Education; 1988.
2. **Dreyfus HL, Dreyfus SE, Athanasiou T.** Mind Over Machine: The Power of Human Intuition and Expertise in the Era of the Computer. New York: Free Pr; 1986.
3. **Shulman LS.** Knowledge and teaching: foundations of the new reform. Harvard Educational Review. 1987;57:1-22.
4. **Shulman LS.** Those who understand: knowledge growth in teaching. Educ Res. 1986; 15:4-14.
5. **Wiese J, ed.** Teaching in the Hospital. Philadelphia: ACP Pr; 2010.
6. **Dewey J.** How We Think, a Restatement of the Relation of Reflective Thinking to the Educative Process. Boston: DC Heath; 1933.
7. **Schön DA.** The Reflective Practitioner: How Professionals Think in Action. New York: Basic Books; 1983.
8. **Gage NL.** The Scientific Basis of the Art of Teaching. New York: Teachers College Pr; 1978.
9. **Ende J, ed.** Theory and Practice of Teaching Medicine. Philadelphia: ACP Pr; 2010.
10. **Skeff KM.** Enhancing teaching effectiveness and vitality in the ambulatory setting. J Gen Intern Med. 1988;3:S26-33.
11. **Litzelman DK, Stratos GA, Marriott DJ, Skeff KM.** Factorial validation of a widely disseminated educational framework for evaluating clinical teachers. Acad Med. 1998; 73:688-95.
12. **Skeff KM, Stratos GA, Berman J, Bergen MR.** Improving clinical teaching. Evaluation of a national dissemination program. Arch Intern Med. 1992;152:1156-61.

2

From Curricular Goals to Instruction: Choosing Methods of Instruction

Patricia A. Thomas, MD, FACP

David E. Kern, MD, MPH

C urricula by definition are planned educational events, and there is a generally agreed-upon process for this planning (1). Every accreditation body in medical education requires that written curricula include *learning objectives, educational methods*, and *evaluation* plans (2–4). To assist in the development of these components, this chapter briefly discusses the following steps in the planning process: conducting a needs assessment, articulating overall goals, developing specific learning objectives, measuring results and, finally, evaluating the curriculum itself. The emphasis of this chapter is on fitting specified methods of teaching, described in subsequent chapters of this book, with curricular goals and objectives. This chapter does not include a complete discussion of evaluation designs; this is covered in greater detail in another book in the *Teaching Medicine* series, *Leadership Careers in Medical Education* (5); readers can consult other references for a more technical discussion of that topic (6).

❖ Needs Assessment

Goals and objectives for a major educational intervention ideally follow a *needs assessment* that identifies and characterizes the health care problem that will be addressed, how it is currently being addressed, and how it should be addressed. At a minimum, the needs

KEY POINTS

- A well-constructed curriculum includes specific and measureable objectives, appropriate methods of instruction to achieve those objectives, and a plan for evaluation of learners and the program.
- Competency-based learner objectives in medical education include knowledge, attitudes, skills, and behavior objectives.
- Methods of instruction should be congruent with curricular objectives and methods of evaluation.
- Choosing the appropriate method of instruction will require knowledge of the learners and of the content and the context in which the learning takes place. This often involves the additional step of performing a needs assessment.
- Many educational theories describe how adults learn; attention to the principles of adult learning theory will improve the efficiency and effectiveness of learning.
- Methods of instruction, as well as evaluation methods, can affect learning environments in both positive and negative ways.

assessment puts the topic into epidemiologic perspective and informs the course director of current versus ideal clinical practice and teaching strategies related to the health care problem. Such information can usually be obtained by reviewing the published literature and selected Internet sites (7) (for example, sites of professional organizations), and by collecting relevant information about one's targeted learners and medical institution (1). For more limited educational activities, such as a single lecture in a pathophysiology course, the needs assessment may focus on the prerequisite learning needed to master the new content to be presented (see also chapter 3 of this book). Examples of the types of needs assessment information that are useful in choosing the goals, objectives, content, and learning methods for one's curriculum include the following:

- For the health care problem: How does it affect patients, health care professionals, medical educators, and society? How does it affect clinical outcomes, quality of life, work and productivity, use and cost of health care and other resources, and societal function? What are the most effective management strategies? How do these compare to current practice?

- For learners and their medical institution: What is the developmental stage of the learners (early clinical students, evolving clinical students, experienced practitioners)? Is there a mix of learners (for example, students, residents, other health professional students)? What are their previous and already planned training in this content area? Is there an opportunity to build on or complement other training? What is known about learners' existing proficiencies and deficiencies, about their preferred learning styles and methods? What is known about the informal or hidden curriculum at their institution (8)? Who are the other stakeholders in the curriculum (for example, course directors, clerkship directors, residency program directors, accrediting bodies), and what are their needs?
- For educators: What are the most effective educational approaches? How do these compare to current approaches? Who will be teaching the curriculum to the targeted learners? Are the teachers content experts? Are they skilled in desired teaching methods? Will faculty development be needed? Are there previously validated evaluation instruments that can be used to evaluate the curriculum?
- Context: What is an appropriate context for learners in which to learn this content? Can more than one context be used to deepen the learning?

Needs assessment methods range from systematic reviews of the medical education literature (9) and formal surveys (10) to informal interviews with groups of learners, faculty, or other stakeholders. The needs assessment provides a foundation for the curriculum that grounds it in best evidence of effectiveness and relevance to the learners. It informs each of the subsequent steps of educational planning: writing goals and objectives, choosing appropriate instructional methods, and planning learner and program evaluation. The needs assessment "makes the argument" for the curriculum, and prepares for needed resources to implement it. A scholarly needs assessment places the curriculum in the context of the educational literature, defines its generalizabilty, and forms the background for its wider dissemination.

❖ Goals

Goals are generally written in broad terms that are easy to communicate to all the stakeholders, including program directors, funding agencies, teachers, and learners. Goals provide desired overall direction for a curriculum.

For example, one goal of a medicine clerkship rotation for medical students may be: *To learn the initial evaluation and management for the most common diagnoses seen on the general internal medicine inpatient service.*

A goal for an intern orientation week program may be: *To teach incoming interns the appropriate patient safety and quality procedures as detailed in the* Hospital Interdisciplinary Clinical Practice Manual.

The following goal could be used for a continuing medical education program: *To provide practicing internists current information and discussion on new developments in cardiovascular medicine.*

❖ Objectives

Determination of methods for instruction should follow from the goals and objectives. If goals are broad and general, objectives are specific and measurable. Objectives can be at the level of the individual learner or the program.

Learner Objectives

Learner objectives focus the curriculum content and inform learners of what is to be achieved. They usually flow from the needs assessment as described in the preceding section. Assuming that the goal of the educational program is to achieve competence in some area of health care, defining that competence usually includes a description of the requisite *knowledge, attitudes,* and *skills* that the learner will need to acquire. Learner objectives then are categorized into three types: cognitive (knowledge), affective (attitudes), and psychomotor (skills or behaviors), often described as the "KAS" framework. These types of objectives are important to note, as you will see later, in choosing the methods of instruction.

Within each type of objective, there is a hierarchy of complexity and achievement. This is most famously described for the cognitive objectives with Bloom's *Taxonomy of Educational Objectives* (11). Bloom's taxonomy lists six levels of cognitive objectives, which not only describe a level of knowledge obtained but also imply the steps of learning required to reach that level. This taxonomy has been revised many times; one of the most recent versions uses the following descriptors of mental tasks: to remember, understand, apply, analyze, evaluate, and create (12). For medical education objectives, for instance, *remembering* factual knowledge (anatomic names for the heart) would be a low-level cognitive objective, whereas *analyzing* an electrocardiogram tracing and the underlying pathophysiology of rhythm disorders would be a higher-level objective. Course directors would want to write the highest expected level of achievement for the learner, otherwise known as the terminal objective. For each event in the course, the objective may describe an enabling objective for this terminal objective. In the example above, a learning objective for the "Cardiovascular Block" course for medical students may be that students will be able to interpret electrocardiogram tracings. A lecture objective within this course may be that learners will be able to explain the normal electrophysiology of the heart.

To ensure that objectives are specific and measurable, it helps to have a template structure for writing the objective. One behavioral method (1) is to structure the objective statement so that it answers the question, "Who will do how much/how well of what by when?" The verbs ("will do") in the objectives describe the behaviors expected of the successful learner, and the nouns ("what") describe the content of the educational program.

Let's say that a workshop is being developed to teach internal medicine interns the proper insertion of central venous catheters. The learner objectives for this workshop could be: *By the end of the 4-hour workshop,*

- *Each intern will be able to cite the risks and complications associated with insertion of central venous catheters.* (Knowledge)
- *Each intern will correctly demonstrate correct procedural steps for insertion of the central venous catheter (as outlined in the observation checklist).* (Skill)
- *Each intern will be committed to minimizing risk for infection during invasive procedures.* (Attitude).

Some considerations in writing learning (or learner) objectives are the following:

- Keep the number of objectives manageable. Too many objectives overwhelm learners and instructors and may diminish the impact of the objectives. This may require combining several similar objectives into one. In the knowledge objective above, "risks and complications" is somewhat general, but it is presumed that several specific risks and complications will be reviewed in the workshop, and that interns will be able to discuss these with patients before the procedure.
- When choosing the verbs for the objectives, use as specific a verb as possible, and one that will imply how the objective will be measured. Verbs such as "will know," "will understand," and "will appreciate" don't necessarily indicate how the objectives will be measured. Table 2-1 shows more useful verbs to use in writing specific measurable objectives.

Table 2-1. Verbs or Phrases for Use in Writing Objectives

Type of Objective	Specific Verbs or Phrases
Cognitive	list, write, recite
	identify
	define
	interpret
	explain
	illustrate
	generate a differential diagnosis, differentiate
	generate a hypothesis
	discriminate
	compare and contrast
	construct
	analyze
	solve
Affective	rate as valuable
	rate as important
	rank as enjoyable
	recognize as having an impact
Psychomotor	demonstrate
	show
	use (in practice)

- Not every curriculum will have all types of objectives. An online curriculum in preventive medicine, for example, could have several knowledge objectives but would be unlikely to have psychomotor objectives.

Program Objectives

What are program objectives and why do we need them? Writing program objectives provides planners with an opportunity to prospectively define the success of the curriculum. Program objectives could simply be written as aggregated learner objectives; for example: "All residents will achieve ≥80% on a knowledge examination at the end of the course." To sustain the curriculum, those developing the curriculum need to know whether the curriculum was implemented as planned. Objectives that address implementation issues are described as *process objectives* for the curriculum. Examples of process objectives include:

- Attendance: *All residents will attend the workshop for its entirety.*
- Participation: *All residents will participate in a role play and debrief with their peers.*
- Functionality: *No resident will report difficulty in logging on to the curriculum Web site.*
- Quality: *Each lecture will be accompanied by detailed lecture notes.*

Many course directors have more ambitious program objectives in mind. These are often termed *outcome* objectives. Some may be conveniently measured, for example:

- Satisfaction: *All residents will report that the role play was a useful method for learning behavioral change counseling.*
- Self-assessed competence: *Residents participating in the workshop will report improved self-efficacy in motivational interviewing techniques.*
- Reported behavior change: *Three months after the workshop, participants, as compared with nonparticipants, will be more likely to report use of the "5As" approach to behavior counseling in their encounters with patients who smoke.*

Other program objectives, such as changes in objectively measured skills, behaviors, or health care outcomes, are more difficult to measure, such as this one:

- Changes in documented resident behaviors and health outcomes: *One year after the course, an audit of patient panels of participant residents will show an increase in documentation of the smoking status of patients and a decline in tobacco use compared with patient panels of nonparticipant residents* (13).

Although sometimes possible to obtain, as in the preceding example, such outcome measurement is frequently not feasible. Nevertheless, the inclusion of some behavioral or health care outcome objectives emphasizes the ultimate aims of a curriculum and should influence the choice of curricular content and educational methods.

❖ Methods of Instruction

Table 2-2 lists the most common methods used in teaching medicine, and subsequent chapters in this book describe several of these methods in more depth. This table highlights the type of objective (and domain) for which each method is best suited, and, for each method, its advantages, its limitations, and the resources required. As noted earlier, the objectives identified through the needs assessment should inform the course director about the most effective method to achieve the goals of the course, but there are

Table 2-2. Common Instructional Methods Used in Teaching Medicine*

Instructional Method: Readings

Objective or Domain
- Knowledge
- Affective

Advantages
- Easily available
- Provides the necessary groundwork in new content for novice learners
- Well-organized and evidence-based
- Can be accessed at optimal time for learners

Limitations
- Passive
- Teacher-centered, since teacher has chosen the material
- If not regulated, may overload learners
- May not be used by learners
- Learning may be superficial, with students relying on short-term memory
- Unlikely to affect long-term knowledge or affect unless paired with another application activity

Faculty and Learner Resources Needed
- Minimal faculty resources
- Online access possible with learning management software or through institutional library electronic reserves
- Need to watch copyright issues, especially in distance-based learning
- Programmed learning requires development

Examples
- Textbooks
- Journals
- Literature (for affective objectives)

Modifications That Enhance Active Learning and Learner-Centeredness
- Programmed learning: learners are intermittently queried about what was just presented and receive feedback (eg, ACP's MKSAP)

Instructional Method: Lecture

Objective or Domain
- Knowledge
- Affective

Table 2-2. Common Instructional Methods Used in Teaching Medicine* (continued)

Advantages

- Provides the groundwork in new content for novice learners
- Presentation software widely available
- Well-organized and evidence-based
- Can be videotaped and reviewed at a later time or online

Limitations

- Passive
- Teacher-centered
- Danger of too much information (i.e., "cognitive overload")
- Limited by attention span of learners
- Learning can be superficial unless paired with another application activity

Faculty and Learner Resources Needed

- Presentation skill development

Examples

- Medicine grand rounds
- House staff noon conference
- Medical student lecture, "Approach to Diabetes Mellitus"

Modifications That Enhance Active Learning and Learner-Centeredness

- Insert activity every 10–15 minutes (e.g., question, discussion with neighbor) (30)

Instructional Method: Discussion Groups

Objective or Domain

- Knowledge and higher cognitive objectives
- Affective

Advantages

- Participatory
- Develops social skills

Limitations

- Learners often need preparatory understanding of content (e.g., reading or prior learning)
- Need time and facilitation to ensure all learners are engaged
- Learners may be frustrated if not skillfully facilitated

Table 2-2. Common Instructional Methods Used in Teaching Medicine* (continued)

Faculty and Learner Resources Needed
- Preparation of materials and facilitation of learners
- Skills of facilitation, such that discussion meets the objectives
- More class time required of learners
- More facilitators required; increased faculty:learner ratio
- If using case-based discussions, may need development of cases and instructors' guides to ensure equivalent experiences across groups

Examples
- Problem sets in a pharmacology course (33)
- Problem-based learning about nutrition in a clinical curriculum (31)
- Journal clubs

Modifications That Enhance Active Learning and Learner-Centeredness
- Problem-based learning (32)
- Team-based learning (34)

Instructional Method: Case Discussion

Objective or Domain
- Knowledge
- Affective
- Skill
- Higher-order objectives of critical thinking, interpreting, and analysis

Advantages
- Embeds learning in the real context of a patient
- Objectives can be adjusted "on the fly" by the faculty discussant
- Learner-centered if learners are allowed to set objectives (i.e., query the expert)
- Including patient perspective facilitates attitudinal and professionalism objectives

Limitations
- Not always available; if relying on available cases for learning, may limit breadth of learning
- Good for auditory learners; may be a problem for other learning preferences
- Team members may have disparate experience and knowledge

Table 2-2. Common Instructional Methods Used in Teaching Medicine* (continued)

Faculty and Learner Resources Needed
- Instructor must possess medical expertise to teach
- Instructor facilitation and bedside teaching skills; should not "take over" the case
- Learner time: If coupled with work rounds, for instance, can impair the workflow for the team
- Paper or virtual cases require development

Examples
- Attending teaching rounds in a medicine clerkship (35)
- Attending rounds on a consultation service (e.g., CDIM SIMPLE online cases)

Modifications That Enhance Active Learning and Learner-Centeredness
- Use "microskills" of clinical teaching (36)
- Set objectives of the discussion by querying learners
- Summarize the discussion when closing it, and negotiate "next steps" in learning

Instructional Method: Demonstration (Modeling)

Objective or Domain
- Skill

Advantages
- Modeling a skill can incorporate other "hidden" objectives, such as patient-centeredness, professionalism (37)

Limitations
- Passive
- Teacher-centered
- Requires that teaching material be available

Faculty and Learner Resources Needed
- Teacher must possess the skill to be demonstrated

Examples
- Bedside cardiovascular examination
- Bedside medical interview
- Teaching knee arthrocentesis

Table 2-2. Common Instructional Methods Used in Teaching Medicine* (continued)

Modifications That Enhance Active Learning and Learner-Centeredness
- Set up the demonstration by clarifying with learners what should be observed
- Summarize the demonstration by asking learners to reflect on what was observed

Instructional Method: Role Play

Objective or Domain
- Affective
- Skill

Advantages
- Active
- Participatory
- Cost-effective, uses learners as the "simulators"
- Learners can appreciate different perspectives when portraying roles

Limitations
- Learners may be resistant (e.g., "I hate acting" or "This doesn't feel real")
- Takes time to set up the role play and debrief effectively

Faculty and Learner Resources Needed
- Faculty facilitation skills
- "Safe" environment that allows learners to take risks and reflect honestly on the experience

Examples
- Smoking cessation curriculum, two residents role-play a physician using motivational interviewing techniques (13)

Modifications That Enhance Active Learning and Learner-Centeredness
- Learner can be invited to set an objective for the role play (e.g., a particular skill he or she would like to try)
- Can be video-recorded for review
- Use "Time Out" technique to get feedback from group members
- Summarize learning points and ask for commitments to change behaviors

Table 2-2. Common Instructional Methods Used in Teaching Medicine* (continued)

Instructional Method: Standardized Patient

Objective or Domain
- Skill
- Affective

Advantages
- Active; participatory
- Standardized patients can be trained to give feedback

Limitations
- Teacher-centered in that the objectives and environment have been created by the teacher
- Learners may be resistant (e.g., "I hate acting" or "This doesn't feel real")
- Standardized patient cases must be developed with checklists, and standardized patients must be trained
- Can be costly; requires standardized patient training time as well as portrayal time

Faculty and Learner Resources Needed
- Trained standardized patients
- Development of standardized patient cases, with validated checklists (38)

Examples
- Medical students learn clinical reasoning with the medical interview (39)
- Practitioners practice motivational interviewing techniques in a smoking cessation workshop (40)

Modifications That Enhance Active Learning and Learner-Centeredness
- Can be videotaped for review by learner or with faculty facilitator
- Incorporating self-assessment can facilitate skill development of self-assessment

Instructional Method: Simulators

Objective or Domain
- Knowledge
- Skill

Table 2-2. Common Instructional Methods Used in Teaching Medicine* (continued)

Advantages
- Active
- Participatory
- Contextual
- "Safe" learning environment; removes anxiety of causing patient harm when learning a skill
- Skill can be practiced with feedback

Limitations
- Not always available
- Can result in negative learning if not carefully developed

Faculty and Learner Resources Needed
- High-tech simulators can be expensive
- Faculty may need training to use effectively
- Instructor:student ratio usually high
- Development of simulator exercises with valid checklists needed

Examples
- "Harvey" cardiac simulator
- "Sim-Man" anesthesia simulator
- Partial task simulators (e.g., vascular access) (41)

Modifications That Enhance Active Learning and Learner-Centeredness
- Using small groups of learners at a time, can incorporate team and communication skills as well as psychomotor skills (42)

Instructional Method: Writing

Objective or Domain
- Knowledge
- Affective
- Higher-order skills of synthesis and analysis, creativity

Advantages
- Active
- Participatory
- Can facilitate habits of reflection
- Embeds and deepens learning

Limitations
- Learners may resist writing and reflection
- If embedded in contact teaching hours, requires time
- Requires skillful introduction

Table 2-2. Common Instructional Methods Used in Teaching Medicine* (continued)

Faculty and Learner Resources Needed
- Time required to do the writing
- Optimal if there is opportunity for learners to receive feedback or discuss

Examples
- Learning portfolios (43)
- Journaling during a substance abuse rotation
- Medical students write about a positive experience with elders in a geriatrics course (44)

Modifications That Enhance Active Learning and Learner-Centeredness
- Follow writing with small-group discussion

Instructional Method: Learning Projects

Objective or Domain
- Knowledge
- Affective
- Skill
- Higher-order skills of analysis, synthesis, and creativity

Advantages
- Active
- Participatory
- Learners can set goals and objectives
- Addresses higher-order skills of analysis and synthesis

Limitations
- Learner resources needed

Faculty and Learner Resources Needed
- Learners need skill in accessing necessary resources
- Time and effort required on part of the learner
- If mentoring is used, high faculty:learner ratio required

Examples
- Residents on the block ambulatory rotation meet as a group to design a practice quality improvement project
- Student groups design and implement a community-based health education project (45)

Modifications That Enhance Active Learning and Learner-Centeredness
- Incorporate self-assessment and reflection
- Incorporate peer evaluation

Table 2-2. Common Instructional Methods Used in Teaching Medicine* (continued)

Instructional Method: Self-Assessment

Objective or Domain
- Attitude
- Skill
- Higher-order skills of analysis

Advantages
- Promotes self-directed and lifelong learning habits

Limitations
- Most effective with mentoring; if not mentored, may be inaccurate and reinforce negative learning

Faculty and Learner Resources Needed
- Faculty mentoring may increase faculty:student ratio
- Both learners and faculty need to be clear about objectives

Examples
- Learning plans developed at the start of a rotation
- Face-to-face feedback that begins with learner self-assessment of progress toward goals
- Learning portfolios (46, 47)

Modifications That Enhance Active Learning and Learner-Centeredness
- Allow objectives for the self-assessment to be set by the learner

Instructional Method: Experiential

Objective or Domain
- Knowledge
- Attitude
- Skill

Advantages
- Contextual; deepens other learning experiences
- Effective in addressing hidden curriculum issues

Limitations
- Not always available
- May not be equivalent for all learners
- Without appropriate debrief, can reinforce negative learning

Table 2-2. Common Instructional Methods Used in Teaching Medicine* (continued)

Faculty and Learner Resources Needed
- High faculty:learner ratio
- Instructors should be aware of modeling opportunities
- Faculty facilitation and debriefing skills
- Learners should be prepared with objectives, some prior knowledge, and observation skills

Examples
- Ambulatory preceptorship for medical students (36)
- Hospice experience in an end-of-life rotation
- Home visit in an internal medicine geriatric rotation (48)

Modifications That Enhance Active Learning and Learner-Centeredness
- Allow goals of the experience to be set by the learner
- Bridge new information to prior knowledge
- Ensure a cogent summarization of the experience with a plan for future learning
- Embed some time for reflection

ACP = American College of Physicians; CDIM = Clerkship Directors in Internal Medicine; MKSAP = Medical Knowledge Self-Assessment Program.

*Numbers in parentheses are reference citations.

several other considerations in choosing an instructional method, including the following list.

1. Instructional methods should be consistent with principles of learning.
2. Instructional methods should be congruent with learner objectives.
3. Multiple instructional methods are better than a single instructional method.
4. Instructional methods can affect the learning environment and have unintended consequences.
5. The choice of methods is often driven by resource limitations.

1. Instructional Methods Should Be Consistent With Principles of Learning

As course directors contemplate potential educational strategies, they should consider principles and issues related to learning, and related to learning by adults in particular. *Teaching* is what educators do, but *learning* is what happens within the learner. The job of teachers, therefore, is largely to *facilitate* learning in curriculum participants. Deeply understood by the ancients, and promulgated by 20th-century educators, is the *andragogic* approach to learning, which is based on the following principles: that adults learn best when they are motivated to learn and set their own goals, when the learning is built on previous experience, and when there are frequent reflection and feedback on how well they are learning (14–16). Learning that promotes the questioning of one's thought processes, behaviors, assumptions, beliefs, and values, along with the consideration of multiple points of view, can result in what has been termed *transformative* learning, which occurs when learners change in meaningful ways (14, 15, 17, 18). Embedding these principles of adult learning into specific instructional methods can improve the efficiency and effectiveness of learning. For instance, a lecture that begins with an application of the concept (for example, case scenarios of disorders of thyroid function) and then presents the concepts (for example, thyroid function), rather than the reverse, is using the principle of motivating learners, by informing them *why* they need to know the concept before presenting the concept. As an example of transformational learning, a video clip showing an interaction with a challenging patient could be used as a trigger tape in a curriculum on managing substance abuse. By promoting reflection and group discussion of learners' assumptions, beliefs, and values, and their potential impact on care, the exercise could promote self-awareness and management of biases in the care of such patients.

A common approach to using andragogic learning principles is the popular "Socratic method" of questioning, often used in hospital teaching rounds (see chapter 1 in *Teaching in the Hospital*, another book in the *Teaching Medicine* series [19]). In this method, the teacher starts with the case (why does the learner needs to learn this), asks a question to determine the learner's previous knowledge or experience, helps the learner to deepen that knowledge with further questioning, and may provide immediate feedback. (Socratic questioning uses simple questions to connect what learners already know, or may know but not appreciate at the moment, and what they need to know to solve a problem. When the instructor ignores the previous knowledge or experience, and asks questions beyond the student's current knowledge base, this is not Socratic questioning. This has been called "pimping," or "tell me what I am thinking," an anxiety-provoking and unproven method of learning [20, 21]). An example of effective Socratic-type questioning follows:

> **Example:** *On the general medical service, Dr. Smith is rounding with Mia and Joe, third-year medical students. Joe has presented his admission from the night before, a patient with cirrhosis and altered mental status.*

Dr. Smith: Mia, this patient is suffering from liver failure. How do we judge the severity of his disease? [Before telling his students how to assess liver function, he is assessing how much they know about assessing liver function]

Mia: I'm not sure. [This student hasn't learned this yet; no point in asking her what the Model for End-Stage Liver Disease (MELD) score is.]

Dr. Smith: Think about the important liver functions. What does the liver do? [Teacher is assessing the limit of her previous knowledge about liver function and failure.]

Mia: It excretes bilirubin in the bile. [Student is remembering basic physiology knowledge; this is the starting point for talking about assessment of liver failure.]

Dr. Smith: Right, so bilirubin levels tell us one indicator of liver function. What else does the liver do?

Mia: It synthesizes coagulation factors.

Dr. Smith: Right, so how can we measure how impaired this function is?

Mia: The INR? [Without additional information transfer, the student has reasoned what one of the important indicators of liver function should be.]

Dr. Smith: Correct. So we can measure serum bilirubin and INR. Joe, what other measures do we have clinically to assess the severity of this patient's liver disease? [Teacher is assuming Joe has done recent reading on this topic because he admitted the patient.]

Joe: The MELD score also includes serum creatinine, since renal dysfunction that happens as a result of ineffective circulation is also a poor prognostic indicator. This patient's MELD score was 23, indicating a 76% mortality in the next 3 months. [Joe has obviously learned the scoring system on his own and is ready to teach others.]

Mia to self: " I didn't know that; I'd better read up on the MELD score." [Mia sets a new learning goal for herself.]

Another way to think of these principles is to decide how learner-centered versus teacher-centered and how active versus passive the method should be. *Teacher-centered* instructional methods allow the instructor to set the learning goals and use an approach that is often the most comfortable for the instructor. The teacher controls the transfer of information. The teacher is usually active and the learner passive, although teacher-centered learning can also be interactive. The classic didactic lecture is an example of a teacher-centered method. Teacher-centered methods may be most appropriate for large numbers of learners or for learners with less previous knowledge or experience in the content area. Some argue that these educational methods do not result in effective learning and are simply "information sharing," a superficial form of learning that results only in short-term memory learning. *Learner-centered* methods imply a flexibility that allows the learners to set learning goals and methods based on previous experience, previous learning, and preferences. This facilitates the process of moving knowledge from short-term memory into a mental model, called a cognitive schema, that allows retrieval of the information when needed (22).

The distinction between teacher- and learner-centered methods is not simplistic, however. Many faculty will introduce active learning strategies into a lecture, for example, that inform learners of how well they are learning or orients the discussion around why they should learn the content. Technology has allowed the adaptation of instructional methods to include more active and more learner-centered approaches. Videotaping lectures and posting them online, for instance, allows learners to access the lecture at a time that is most conducive for the learner to listen. In many instances, learners can pace the information that is given in the lecture, listening in double-time for parts that are easily understood, and stopping and repeating for parts of the lecture that need more time. Interactivity of the learner with a computer program, with intermittent self-assessment questions, informs the learners of how well they are learning. The use of audience response systems is another method of increasing learner-centeredness. The lecturer may insert questions periodically in the lecture and ask participants to respond; by looking at the responses from the group as a whole, it may be apparent to the lecturer that some material needs to be explained again or with another approach. Subsequent chapters in this book will explain how methods can be enhanced to address principles of adult learning and learner-centeredness.

Going beyond the principles of adult learning, transformational learning, and learner-centeredness, many educational theories attempt to describe how we learn, and therefore suggest optimal instructional methods. Major theories in use in medical education are the behavioral learning, the cognitive learning, the humanist, the social learning, and the constructivist theories (analogous to the experiential theory of learning described in chapter 1 of *Theory and Practice of Teaching Medicine* [23]) (24). Table 2-3 briefly defines these theories and provides example instructional methods that are supported by them (see also chapter 2 in *Theory and Practice of Teaching Medicine*).

Table 2-3. Educational Theories Supporting Instructional Methods

Educational Theory: Behavioral Learning Theory

Definition
- Learning is the acquisition of observable behaviors that occur through conditioning. Objectives are written as observable behaviors. The teacher controls the environment and provides feedback.

Type/Domain Objective
- Competency
- Behavior change in a practitioner

Medical Education Example
- Simulations: Practicing the correct procedures of running a code team, receiving feedback
- Direct observation of the medical interview: Practicing open-ended questions in a medical interview course; receiving feedback

Educational Theory: Constructivist (Experiential) (49)

Definition
- Learning is an active process by which the learner is constructing meaning from new sensory input (i.e., integrating experiences into previously held knowledge and beliefs). The teacher facilitates the mental task involved in constructing meaning, such as reflection on an experience.

Type/Domain Objective
- Knowledge
- Affective
- Skill/competency

Medical Education Example
- Activities that incorporate reflection, such as:
  - Listening to a physician–patient interview and reflecting on the patient's perspective
  - Debriefing a code team's performance
  - Examining a patient with a neurologic lesion and relating it to previously learned neuroanatomy

Educational Theory: Social Learning Theory (50)

Definition
- Learning occurs through observing behaviors of others and the outcomes of those behaviors. Methods include observation, imitation, and modeling. The steps in learning are attention, retention, reproduction, and motivation. The teacher is a role model.

continued

Table 2-3. Educational Theories Supporting Instructional Methods (continued)

Type/Domain Objective
- Competency

Medical Education Example
- One-on-one clinical teaching, such as an ambulatory preceptorship: A medical student observes a clinician screening for alcohol abuse, imitates it successfully, and incorporates it into future practice

Educational Theory: Humanism (51)

Definition
- Learning occurs as a mechanism of self-actualization and self-fulfillment. Affective and cognitive needs are addressed through learning; the teacher is a facilitator.

Type/Domain Objective
- Cognitive
- Affective

Medical Education Example
- Activities that encourage self-directed learning and self-assessment, such as learning projects and learning portfolios
- Discussion groups that allow learners to explore new ideas, set their own learning objectives, and find new information on their own, such as problem-based learning

Educational Theory: Cognitivist (22)

Definition
- Learning results from inferences and making connections with prior knowledge. Knowledge is seen as symbolic mental structures. Learning involves the active process of moving information from short-term memory into knowledge structures. Instruction should be structured and well-organized with feedback to the learners.

Type/Domain Objective
- Knowledge
- Higher-order cognitive objectives

Medical Education Example
- Information transfer followed by activities that encourage synthesis, analysis, and higher-order cognitive skills, such as:
  - Renal failure lecture followed by team work to generate differential diagnoses for diagnostic dilemmas
  - Creating maps, tables, or other memory aids to facilitate retrieval of knowledge

*Numbers in parentheses are reference citations.

2. Instructional Methods Should Be Congruent With Learner Objectives

Learning is contextual—what is learned in one situation is not always transferred to a different context. A student may "learn" the pathophysiology of congestive heart failure by attending a lecture, but may not recognize that pathophysiology when seeing a patient in clinic. Effective teaching methods often present material in the same context in which the learner will need this learning. Attention to the verbs used in the learner objectives is again helpful here.

Let's take the objectives written for the intern workshop on central venous catheterization. Because the intent of the workshop is to improve patient care, the best instructional methods will allow interns to practice the behaviors that would be used in patient care. The first objective, that interns *will be able to cite* the risks and complications of central venous catheterization, could be learned in a lecture, or by reading, but will be much more powerful if the intern is then required to "*cite* the risks" in a *role play* discussion of informed consent with a patient. Similarly, the correct procedural steps could be introduced through a video or demonstration, but the psychomotor skill is best learned by practice and feedback with a *simulator*, that is, allowing the learner to "*demonstrate* the correct procedure." As a rule, some instructional methods are more useful in achieving certain types of objectives (Table 2-2).

3. Multiple Instructional Methods Are Better Than a Single Method

This principle addresses the reality that learners have a variety of learning preferences or learning styles (25). Having more than one method improves the likelihood that significant learning will occur. In addition, using more than one method allows reinforcement of the learning without the appearance of redundancy, and deepens learning by practicing in different contexts. For example, let's say the goal of a short curriculum is that medical students will learn proper hospital infection-control procedures. The methods could include an online curriculum that introduces the appropriate protective equipment and procedures for infection control with a video. After watching the video, students practice gowning in small groups, and simulating sterile technique with a partial task simulator, such as lumbar puncture.

4. Instructional Methods Affect the Learning Environment and Can Have Unintended Consequences

Instructional methods can convey messages to learners that are more powerful than the content of the curriculum. To say that a curriculum is designed to develop critical thinkers and lifelong learners and then rely heavily on lecture methods that do not address these objectives may result in learners who devalue those objectives. Using frequent individual assessments to drive learning can create competition and thwart the development of team and social skills. On the other hand, embedding reflection and self-assessment into instructional methods may facilitate habits of reflection and self-directed, autonomous learners. Providing opportunities to work in teams and to assess team skills encourages development of team skills as well as providing meaningful experiences for the learning. In general, following the principles above will result in an effective curriculum that conveys respect for the learners and fosters professional values.

5. The Choice of Methods Is Often Driven by Resource Limitations

Major resource issues include space (facilities use), technical costs (paper, software, computer stations), development costs, faculty time, and learner time, all of which may force the choice of one method over another. Students generally enjoy simulations and report good learning, but simulations may be expensive to develop and run, and the simulators are not always available. Discussions require more curricular time and faculty facilitators than lectures do. Some affective objectives, such as cultural competence, may be effectively addressed by faculty role modeling of appropriate behaviors, but that requires a critical mass of trained faculty modeling these behaviors. A significant learner resource is time. Table 2-2 provides information on resources required for different methods. The course director often must balance what is ideal (on the basis of one's needs assessment and application of the above principles) with what is feasible. Understanding the ideal, however, can stimulate the development of innovative, creative approaches that are feasible, such as the team-based learning method developed as a method of integrating small-group discussions into the context of large class sizes (26).

❖ Evaluation

Evaluation is an important step in the educational process that benefits from thoughtful planning. This chapter focuses on the uses of evaluation and the choice of evaluation methods. It does not specifically discuss evaluation design, the reliability and validity of measurement instruments, data analysis, evaluation reports, or ethical concerns. Rigorous evaluations can become quite sophisticated. If they become foci for dissemination or publication, they are considered educational research and require consultation with one's institutional review board. As mentioned earlier, a more detailed discussion of evaluation, both programmatic and learner-specific, can be found in *Leadership Careers in Medical Education* (5), as well as other references (6).

An important consideration in planning for an evaluation is to clarify how the evaluation will be used. Is it critical to demonstrate learner competence, as in such certification courses as advanced cardiac life support? Do learners have a need to know whether they have achieved the objectives? Or is the major concern for the course director to know that the program objective was achieved, as in continuing medical education courses? Can the evaluation be embedded in another evaluation plan (for example, one lecture's evaluation may occur in the end of course examination)? Are there an interest in disseminating the curriculum or justifying its resources and a need to document its effectiveness? Evaluation plans range from simple to elaborate; understanding how the evaluation will be used allows the planners to prioritize evaluation methods. Table 2-4 provides a general framework for an evaluation plan.

Just as *objectives* are written at the learner level and at the program level, *evaluations* are usually planned at the learner and the program levels (additional discussion of this topic is provided in *Leadership Careers in Medical Education* [5]). Curricula with the most impact inform learners how they are doing during the course (*formative evaluation* with feedback) as well as whether they have achieved objectives at the end of the course (*summative evaluation* with feedback). It is helpful to remember that formative evaluation methods that are administered to learners during a curriculum also serve as methods of instruction.

Considerations listed above for deciding on instructional methods also apply to decisions regarding the choice of evaluation methods. *Evaluation methods should be consistent with the principles of adult learning.* In keeping with these principles, feedback from effective evaluations is specific and constructive and provides learners with information that allows

Table 2-4. Levels and Generic Uses of Evaluation

Generic Use	Level	
	Individual Learner	**Program**
Formative	Is the learner making progress in achieving the objectives? How can the learner improve performance?	Are all learners making progress in achieving the objectives? How can the program be improved?
Summative	Did the learner achieve the objectives? How well?	Did all learners achieve the objectives? Did the program achieve its process and outcome objectives?

them to set the next personal learning goal. Using a standardized patient assessment that just provides students with a checklist score does not help them understand how to improve their performance. On the other hand, modern online software for knowledge testing can allow learners not only to see a final score immediately but also review the items answered incorrectly, and plan for further study. Once again, it is important to maintain congruence with the objectives and instructional methods. If objectives are specific and measurable, the learner evaluations will flow easily. For example, if the goal of the educational event is acquisition of a skill, it would be inappropriate to assess learning with a written examination; rather, an appropriate measurement would be to assess the acquisition of the skill by observing learners' performance with simulators, standardized or real patients. Table 2-5 provides information on various evaluation methods and their uses, advantages, and limitations.

Because no measurement is perfect, the most valid assessments use the strategy of "multiple measures by multiple observers at multiple points of time." This may be feasible for major competencies, such as communication or clinical reasoning, or in long curricula, such as a residency training program, where there may be multiple opportunities for learner assessment.

Table 2-5. Common Evaluation Methods, Uses, Advantages, and Limitations

Method: Global Rating Forms

Uses
- Knowledge, attitude, skill
- Objectives
- Formative and summative

Advantages
- Easy to distribute and complete
- Frequently used online

Limitations
- Subjective
- Rater biases (halo effect)
- Limited inter-rater reliability because scales are interpreted differently
- Contextual information is lacking

Method: Multisource Feedback

Uses
- Knowledge, attitude, skill
- Objectives
- Formative and summative

continued

Table 2-5. Common Evaluation Methods, Uses, Advantages, and Limitations (continued)

Advantages
- Rich context from multiple observers increases validity
- Open text can generate good qualitative information

Limitations
- Resource intensive to develop appropriate instruments, distribute, collect, analyze, and communicate results
- Not all respondents (such as patients) can be trained as evaluators

Method: Self-Assessment Forms

Uses
- Knowledge, attitude, skill
- Objectives
- Formative and summative

Advantages
- Easy to distribute and complete

Limitations
- Subjective
- Rater biases
- Correlation with objective measures has been historically low
- Considered the least rigorous form of learner assessment

Method: Questionnaires

Uses
- Attitude, skill, and performance
- Objectives
- Formative and summative

Advantages
- Easy to distribute and complete
- Can generate quantitative data

Limitations
- Subjective
- Responses can be influenced by social desirability
- Requires moderate resources to develop validated tools

Method: Focus Groups

Uses
- Knowledge, attitudes, skill
- Formative and summative
- Program evaluation

continued

Table 2-5. Common Evaluation Methods, Uses, Advantages, and Limitations (continued)

Advantages
- Qualitative
- Can generate pertinent items for questionnaires
- Can develop "theory" to be further tested

Limitations
- Requires expertise in resources to facilitate the focus group and analyze the results
- Results may depend on participation, which could be biased

Method: Written Tests (multiple-choice exams)

Uses
- Knowledge, objectives
- Formative and summative

Advantages
- Can achieve good psychometric properties, with internal reliability
- Software can assist in mapping to complex curricula
- Generates quantitative data that help in making decisions about performance

Limitations
- Reliable tests require resources for development and psychometric testing
- Resources required for administration and scoring and communication to learners

Method: Written Essay

Uses
- Knowledge, affective, and skill objectives
- Formative and summative

Advantages
- Provides opportunities to demonstrate higher cognitive objectives, such as reasoning
- Provides opportunities to demonstrate habits of reflection
- Provides a rich context for setting future learning goals

Limitations
- Rater biases in scoring
- Requires qualitative methods and resources to analyze

Method: Oral Examinations

Uses
- Knowledge, especially higher cognitive objectives, such as clinical reasoning
- When scored, usually summative

continued

Table 2-5. Common Evaluation Methods, Uses, Advantages, and Limitations (continued)

Advantages
  • Face validity

Limitations
  • Rater biases
  • Subjective scoring

Method: Direct Observation

Uses
  • Skill and behavior objectives
  • Formative and summative

Advantages
  • If using checklists, trained observers can provide reliable and objective results

Limitations
  • Requires development of checklists, opportunities for observation (simulated or real), and trained observers (faculty)
  • Can be resource intensive

Method: Logs

Uses
  • Skill and behavior objectives

Advantages
  • Objective
  • Documents real-life experience
  • Can be tool for reflection

Limitations
  • Only as valid as learner entries
  • Electronic entry can help with analysis, but otherwise resource intensive to analyze

Method: Performance Audits

Uses
  • Skill and behavior objectives

Advantages
  • High face validity
  • Can generate quantitative data
  • Can be a tool for reflection and self-directed learning

Limitations
  • Depends on available data sources and what is reliably recorded; misses what is not documented

The multiplicity of data points increases the reliability and validity of the assessment. For such programs or in high-stakes situations, planners should consult additional resources on evaluation design and psychometrics. Reliability and validity are less critical for shorter educational events, such as a bedside teaching encounter, lecture, or workshop.

One model of learner assessment in medical student education has been Miller's pyramid (27) (Figure 2-1). As learners advance in expertise, they pass through the following stages: "knows," "knows how," "shows how," and, finally, "does." The model allows an ultimate objective to be the incorporation of certain behaviors into clinical practice. Ideally, the evaluation should aim to assess the highest point of the pyramid that is appropriate for the level of learner and objectives of the educational program. Medical education curricula are faulted for not designing assessments that address the "shows how" (assessment of skill) and "does" (behavior in clinical practice) levels of skill because it is assumed that competence at these levels is more likely to affect patient outcomes (28). Usually, however, the higher the point on the pyramid, the more resource-intensive the evaluation.

Resource limitations are also a consideration in designing evaluations. Course planners may not have the resources of standardized patients or high-tech simulations. If the goal of the evaluation is to support educational research, the evaluation plan will aim for the highest level in a hierarchy of designs from pretest/post-test comparisons to randomized, controlled

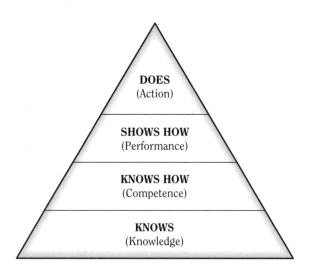

Figure 2-1 Framework for clinical assessment. Reproduced with permission from Miller GE. The assessment of clinical skills/competence/performance. Acad Med. 1990;65:S63-S67.

trials. Ethical issues, such as just allocation of curricular time and resources and confidentiality, should also be considered.

There is perhaps no element of an educational event that affects the learning environment more than the evaluation plan. The educational truism "Assessment drives learning" makes the point that what is evaluated is what learners will strive to achieve. For example, an evaluation that tests knowledge objectives but ignores interpersonal skill development objectives communicates that knowledge is more valued than interpersonal skills. Evaluations that include peer assessments appear to foster professionalism (29). How much time is devoted to evaluation rather than learning, what kind of learning is evaluated (factual knowledge vs. critical thinking skills), scoring systems (satisfactory/unsatisfactory vs. number grades), communication and confidentiality of results, will all affect the learning environment.

❖ Summary

Internists teach in a variety of situations, from the lecture hall with large audiences to precepting in the clinic with a single trainee. Whether planning for a complex curriculum or preparing for hospital rounds, the quality of an educational experience can be enhanced by the processes outlined in this chapter: assessing needs, articulating goals and objectives, considering the optimal methods to achieve those objectives, assessing achievement of the objectives, and reviewing the evaluation results available to the teacher. But the process of moving from curricular goals to methods of instruction is not a line, with a beginning and an end; rather, it is a loop, in which evaluation informs further curricular and instructional decisions and so on. The most creative teaching often involves rethinking goals and methods. Refining the specific methods of instruction will be discussed in subsequent chapters.

REFERENCES

1. **Kern DE, Thomas PA, Hughes MT, eds.** Curriculum Development in Medical Education: A Six-Step Approach. 2nd ed. Baltimore: Johns Hopkins Univ Pr; 2009.
2. **Liaison Committee on Medical Education.** Functions and Structure of a Medical School. 2009. Accessed at www.lcme.org.
3. **Accreditation Council for Graduate Medical Education.** Common program requirements. Accessed at www.acgme.org.
4. **Accreditation Council for Continuing Medical Education.** Accreditation requirements. Accessed at www.accme.org.
5. **Pangaro L, ed.** Leadership Careers in Medical Education. Philadelphia: ACP Pr; 2010.
6. **Lipsett P, Kern DE.** Step 6: Evaluation and Feedback. Curriculum Development in Medical Education: A Stepwise Approach. Baltimore: Johns Hopkins Univ Pr; 2009.

7. **Thomas PA, Kern DE.** Internet resources for curriculum development in medical education: an annotated bibliography. J Gen Intern Med. 2004;19:599-605.
8. **Hundert EM, Hafferty F, Christakis D.** Characteristics of the informal curriculum and trainees' ethical choices. Acad Med. 1996;71:624-42.
9. **Littlewood S, Ypinazar V, Margolis SA, Scherpbier A, Spencer J, Dornan T.** Early practical experience and the social responsiveness of clinical education: systematic review. BMJ. 2005;331:387-91.
10. **Elnicki DM, van Londen J, Hemmer PA, Fagan M, Wong R.** U.S. and Canadian internal medicine clerkship directors' opinions about teaching procedural and interpretive skills to medical students. Acad Med. 2004;79:1108-13.
11. **Bloom BS.** Taxonomy of Educational Objectives: A Classification of Educational Objectives. Handbook 1: Cognitive Domain. New York: Longman; 1984.
12. **Anderson L, Krathwohl DR.** A Taxonomy for Learning, Teaching, and Assessing: A Revision of Bloom's Taxonomy of Educational Objectives. New York: Addison Wesley Longman; 2001.
13. **Cornuz J, Humair JP, Seematter L, Stoianov R, van Melle G, Stalder H, et al.** Efficacy of resident training in smoking cessation: a randomized, controlled trial of a program based on application of behavioral theory and practice with standardized patients. Ann Intern Med. 2002;136:429-37.
14. **Knowles M.** Androgagy in Action. San Francisco: Jossey-Bass; 1984.
15. **Schön D.** Educating the Reflective Practitioner. San Francisco: Jossey-Bass; 1987.
16. **Brookfield S.** Adult Learning: An Overview. International Encyclopedia of Education. Oxford, United Kingdom: Pergamon Pr; 1995.
17. **Rogers C.** Significant Learning in Therapy and Education. On Becoming a Person: A Therapist's View of Psychotherapy. Boston: Houghton-Mifflin; 1961:279-96.
18. **Mezirow J.** Transformative Dimensions of Adult Learning. San Francisco: Jossey-Bass; 1991.
19. **Wiese J, ed.** Teaching in the Hospital. Philadelphia: ACP Pr; 2010.
20. **Detsky AS.** The art of pimping. JAMA. 2009;301:1379-81.
21. **Wear D, Kokinova M, Keck-McNulty C, Aultman J.** Pimping: perspectives of 4th year medical students. Teach Learn Med. 2005;17:184-91.
22. **Baddeley AD, Hitch GJ.** Working Memory. In: Bower G, ed. The Psychology of Learning and Motivation in Research and Theory. New York: Academic Pr; 1974:47-89.
23. **Ende J, ed.** Theory and Practice of Teaching Medicine. Philadelphia: ACP Pr; 2010.
24. **Torre DM, Daley BJ, Sebastian JL, Elnicki DM.** Overview of current learning theories for medical educators. Am J Med. 2006;119:903-7.
25. **Chapman DM, Calhoun JG.** Validation of learning style measures: implications for medical education practice. Med Educ. 2006;40:576-83.
26. **Michaelsen L, Knight AB, Fink LD.** Team-Based Learning: A Transformative Use of Small Groups in College Teaching. Sterling, VA: Stylus; 2004.
27. **Miller GE.** The assessment of clinical skills/competence/performance. Acad Med. 1990; 65:S63-7.
28. **Kassebaum DG, Eaglen RH.** Shortcomings in the evaluation of students' clinical skills and behaviors in medical school. Acad Med. 1999;74:842-9.
29. **Epstein RM, Dannefer EF, Nofziger AC, Hansen JT, Schultz SH, Jospe N, et al.** Comprehensive assessment of professional competence: the Rochester experiment. Teach Learn Med. 2004;16:186-96.
30. **Brown G, Manogue M.** AMEE Medical Education Guide No. 22: Refreshing lecturing: a guide for lecturers. Med Teach. 2001;23:231-244.

31. **Marin-Campos Y, Mendoza-Morales L, Navarro-Hernández JA.** Students' assessment of problems in a problem-based learning pharmacology course. Adv Health Sci Educ Theory Pract. 2004;9:299-307.
32. **O'Neill PA.** The role of basic sciences in a problem-based learning clinical curriculum. Med Educ. 2000;34:608-13.
33. **Wood DF.** Problem based learning. BMJ. 2003;326:328-30.
34. **Thompson BM, Schneider VF, Haidet P, Levine RE, McMahon KK, Perkowski LC, et al.** Team-based learning at ten medical schools: two years later. Med Educ. 2007;41:250-7.
35. **Kilminster S, Cottrell D, Grant J, Jolly B.** AMEE Guide No. 27: Effective educational and clinical supervision. Med Teach. 2007;29:2-19.
36. **Neher JO, Gordon KC, Meyer B, Stevens N.** A five-step "microskills" model of clinical teaching. J Am Board Fam Pract. 1992;5:419-24.
37. **Cruess RL.** Teaching professionalism: theory, principles, and practices. Clin Orthop Relat Res. 2006;449:177-85.
38. **Bosek MS, Li S, Hicks FD.** Working with standardized patients: a primer. Int J Nurs Educ Scholarsh. 2007;4:Article 16.
39. **Windish DM, Price EG, Clever SL, Magaziner JL, Thomas PA.** Teaching medical students the important connection between communication and clinical reasoning. J Gen Intern Med. 2005;20:1108-13.
40. **Francis N, Rollnick S, McCambridge J, Butler C, Lane C, Hood K.** When smokers are resistant to change: experimental analysis of the effect of patient resistance on practitioner behaviour. Addiction. 2005;100:1175-82.
41. **Ault MJ, Rosen BT, Ault B.** The use of tissue models for vascular access training. Phase I of the procedural patient safety initiative. J Gen Intern Med. 2006;21:514-7.
42. **Grantcharov TP, Reznick RK.** Teaching procedural skills. BMJ. 2008;336:1129-31.
43. **Feigelson S, Muller D.** "Writing About Medicine": an exercise in reflection at Mount Sinai (with five samples of student writing). Mt Sinai J Med. 2005;72:322-32.
44. **Westmoreland GR, Counsell SR, Sennour Y, Schubert CC, Frank KI, Wu J, et al.** Improving medical student attitudes toward older patients through a "council of elders" and reflective writing experience. J Am Geriatr Soc. 2009;57:315-20.
45. **Averill NJ, Sallee JM, Robinson JT, McFarlin JM, Montgomery AA, Burkhardt GA, et al.** A first-year community-based service learning elective: design, implementation, and reflection. Teach Learn Med. 2007;19:47-54.
46. **Farnill D, Hayes SC, Todisco J.** Interviewing skills: self-evaluation by medical students. Med Educ. 1997;31:122-7.
47. **Chisholm CD, Croskerry P.** A case study in medical error: the use of the portfolio entry. Acad Emerg Med. 2004;11:388-92.
48. **Hervada-Page M, Fayock KS, Sifri R, Markham FW Jr.** The home visit experience: a medical student's perspective. Care Manag J. 2007;8:206-10.
49. **Bruner J.** The Process of Education. 2nd ed. Cambridge, MA: Harvard Univ Pr; 1977.
50. **Bandura A.** Social Learning Theory. New York: General Learning Pr; 1977.
51. **Stern DT, Cohen JJ, Bruder A, Packer B, Sole A.** Teaching humanism. Perspect Biol Med. 2008;51:495-507.

3

The Lecture: Tips to Make Your Next Presentation Go Better Than Your Last

Scott C. Litin, MD, MACP

Jack Ende, MD, MACP

As physicians we are often asked to present lectures to colleagues, students, house staff, the public, and even patients. Though the settings may differ, the skill sets needed for effective outcomes are remarkably similar. Chapter 2 identified the educational purposes for which the lecture is best suited, and compared the lecture with other instructional methods, such as seminars, workshops, or case discussions. This chapter focuses on how to prepare and deliver an effective lecture. This traditional method has not, as many educational theorists predicted, been "consigned to the graveyard of academic history" to be replaced by more learner-centered, less directive techniques. In fact, the lecture lives on. As a means to introduce information, particularly when concepts are complex or interrelated in ways that may not immediately be clear, to introduce alternate perspectives or interpretations, to model attitudes or to encourage thinking, a well-done lecture may be the technique of choice. Moreover, in academic medicine, where lectures provide a social function, whether it be convening a department for Grand Rounds, introducing a visiting professor, or providing continuing medical education, it is safe to say the lecture is here to stay.

Teachers' reputations are intimately tied to their success as lecturers. Indeed, lecturing is important to most academic medical professionals; careers may depend on how we present ourselves and

---

KEY POINTS

- The lecture remains an effective teaching technique, and for several reasons, in several situations, it remains the technique of choice.
- Lectures should be prepared with specific purposes in mind, principally to meet the needs of your audience— that is, what they want to know or need to know about your topic, not simply what you want to tell them.
- Presentations should have a powerful opening statement to hook the audience, emphasize only a limited number of points, and provide a strong closing.
- The lecturer should be concerned with the actual presentation, that is, make it a performance—smile, be enthusiastic, use pauses, illustrate your points with stories and pictures—and appreciate the differences in what is asked of an audience when they learn from a lecture versus learning from other modalities, such as reading.
- Practice is highly valuable, including practicing out loud, to make your next presentation better than your last.

---

our information when we speak to colleagues, students, patients, and the public. Moreover, by enhancing the learning of others, good lecturers improve the effectiveness of the profession as a whole.

This chapter provides an approach to organizing and delivering a lecture. The goal here is to highlight the strategies and tactics that can help you make your next lecture better than the last. Four sections are presented. The first three sections address the following: 1) how to organize the content of the lecture (that is, determining what is important for your audience to hear); 2) how to present yourself and your material (because effective lecturing depends so much on the lecturer's performance); and 3) how to most effectively use audiovisuals (including PowerPoint). The fourth section brings this all together with some practical tips and words of wisdom. Throughout the chapter, the terms "presentation," "talk," and "lecture" are used interchangeably. The recommendations made in this chapter are based on a synthesis of personal experiences derived from listening to and critiquing over 1000 presentations, reviewing thousands of continuing medical education evaluation forms on speakers, as well as the educational literature on this topic.

❖ Getting Organized

As indicated in Box 3-1, there is a sequence of questions presenters should consider as they begin to plan their talk. Even before asking the "what" question ("What will I say?"), the "who" question ("Who will be listening?"), or the "how" question ("How in the world will I ever pull this off?"), the effective lecturer needs to ask "why". Often ignored, but crucial in how it can direct preparation and presentation, the "why" question asks, "Why did they [the course director, the residency program director, my chair, the American College of Physicians Program Planning Committee, or my colleague from 10 years ago] ask me to do this?" Is the lecture part of a course, in which case the lecturer needs to know what came before and what will follow? Is the lecture part of a series, in which case the lecturer needs to understand just what the host has in mind? Or is the lecturer invited as a guest speaker, in which case his or her principal goal might be to provide a stimulating educational hour and, it is hoped, get invited back. Lectures are given for any of several purposes. The point here is, don't guess. The lecturer needs to know why this lecture is happening, and even why she or he was invited to give this particular talk. Only then can the intended outcomes, content, format, and style be considered.

Related to "why" is "who." Who will the audience be? What do they already know about this topic? What are their biases? And what do they *need* to know? Teachers may unconsciously be working from what some have called the "banking" concept of education, in which lecturers assume learners' minds are like empty vaults waiting for knowledge to be deposited; the larger the deposit, the more valuable the lecture. Simply put, that's wrong. Lecturers should be working from the framework that their learn-

---

Box 3-1. Questions to Help Organize a Lecture

- ▶ Why is this talk being presented?
- ▶ What do I hope to achieve with this talk?
- ▶ What do the learners already know and need to know?
- ▶ What are my three to five most important points?
- ▶ How can I support, prove, and illustrate each point?
- ▶ How can I ensure that the audience will stay on track with me?
- ▶ How will I open?
- ▶ How will I close?

ers already have at least some knowledge of the topic but that their knowledge needs to be further developed, reshaped, or even reconstructed.

Armed now with an understanding of why the lecture is happening, who the audience is, and what their needs are, the lecturer can then tackle the "what" question: What information should be included? A useful rule of thumb is that a 40-minute lecture should develop no more than three to five major points. This small number of major points can be the basis for the outline. The lecturer needs to be disciplined because it is so easy to drift toward information overload, cramming far too much material into a talk. On the other hand, limiting the talk to three to five of the most salient points allows for a more interesting and engaging lecture. The major points can be foreshadowed at the beginning of the talk, developed further in the body of the talk, and summarized at the end. Trite though it may be, the old adage "Tell them what you are going to tell them, tell them, and tell them what you told them" remains useful advice.

Similarly, the advice "begin at the end and end at the beginning" provides an organizational structure that helps lecturers prepare their outlines and deliver their talks. Work back from the major points, building a case for each, and decide what information, illustrations, graphics, and so forth will guide the audience toward the major points. Here is where quotes, anecdotes, and stories—the more personal, the better—come into play. The order of the major points, as well as how they are linked, make up the final considerations in organizing the talk.

❖ Presenting the Lecture—and Yourself

Appearances do count. Particularly if the lecturer is a guest from an outside institution, dress, demeanor, and posture are all important, as is the speaker's level of energy and enthusiasm. The speaker who bounds up to the podium, smiling, ready to take charge, creates one type of first impression; the speaker who nervously slinks to the lectern, looking scared, and introduces himself or herself with a fumbling apology designed to enlist the audience's forgiveness rather than their respect creates an impression that is totally different. Regardless of one's personal style, enthusiasm and taking charge are not wrong; fact, they're expected.

Along these same lines, it is important to appreciate the difference between communicating in writing (with a chapter, for instance) and communicating in words. Readers can go back, check, refresh their memory about a complex point, scan figures at their own pace, and even set the chapter down. Learners in a lecture can do none of this. So it is important for speakers to communicate deliberately, offering a measured amount of material, paced to enable the learner to keep up. Sign posts are important. Comments or slides that announce "Here is where we are; here is where we are going" allow listeners to stay on track and to get back on track if they might have drifted off.

It is also important to appreciate that the lecture is a performance. Do not be so casual as to turn your lecture into a chat. "Be yourself" is always sound advice, but remember as well to be your most professional self. In that same vein, the question often arises, Should lectures be memorized or read from texts? Yes, they should be performances. But no, they should not follow a script. True, that is how many eloquent presidential speeches are delivered. So what about a lecture to a medical audience? For the latter, where the goal is to reach (hopefully) a few hundred learners rather than set down for the record an address intended to reach the entire Free World, speaking rather than reading is preferred. The best lectures are more organized than casual conversation but retain a conversational tone. Lectures that are read can come across as stilted. Audiences wonder whether it would be easier to read the text themselves. Eye contact between speaker and audience suffers as the lecturer buries his nose in his notes, or turns his head to the screen. While accomplished orators can stir audiences by reading a well-crafted speech from a prepared text, the rest of us probably are more effective performing from notes.

❖ Using Audiovisuals

Effective Use of the Microphone
It helps to get comfortable with a lavalier microphone. With this type of microphone, the power source attaches to your belt and the microphone piece runs on a thin cord that can be attached to your tie, blouse, or lapel. This permits you the move away from the lectern, thus allowing for visible body language and a better connection with the audience. However, when wearing a lavalier microphone, do not have the power source near your cell phone or pager even if those devices are in the silent vibration mode. Even when silent, activated pagers or cell phones will create electrical interference with the lavalier microphone, which causes irritating static noises over the speaker system. Therefore, it is best to turn cell phones and pagers off if they are on your body or, better yet, not wear them at all when you are speaking. Finally, women using lavalier microphones should wear clothing that will allow the microphone to be attached close to the center (men usually have the advantage of attaching it to their tie). Women should also watch out for physical interference from long hair or a scarf brushing the top of the microphone. Foreign objects rubbing against the top of the

microphone create an unpleasant scratchy noise that is distracting to the audience.

PowerPoint Issues

In the 21st century, presentations with PowerPoint have become the norm. PowerPoint often can add to your presentation, but sometimes it can detract. Audiences universally complain about several issues with PowerPoint-driven presentations:

- Speakers reading their slides word for word
- Speakers who face the projection screen reading slides or who stare only at the computer screen, as opposed to making eye contact with the audience
- Too much information on slides. It is important to remember the rule of six when you are preparing text slides: Try to avoid any more than six bulleted items per text slide and more than six words per line.
- Slides consisting entirely of full sentences or, worse yet, cut-and-paste paragraphs

The background of PowerPoint slides is important. Avoid using background images on your slides because they are very distracting and make the text much more difficult to read. Make sure the colors you use are visible, clear, and nondistracting to the audience. It has been suggested that a blue background for slides is most pleasant and easy to read. Use white for text and highlight in yellow on a blue background. Reds and greens are problematic. While these colors look good on the computer screen, they may not project well for most audience members, not just those who are color blind. Many speakers use red to highlight important words on their slides; in reality, however, this makes the image less visible to the reader and actually "lowlights" instead of highlights the word.

The type size of your title heading should be anywhere from 36 to 44 points and the text between 24 and 32 points. The latter size is easier for the audiences to read and also prevents you from overloading your slides. San serif fonts (Arial or Helvetica) are easier for the audience to interpret. Serif fonts (such as Times New Roman) have extra projections or finishing strokes on the letters and make it more difficult for the audience to read the words on the slides. Avoid all uppercase letters because these take longer for the audience to read. Uppercase can be used to EMPHASIZE specific words in the text as an alternative to a color (yellow).

Moving, spinning, and flying text using custom animation can be very distracting and should be used sparingly. In contrast, the custom animation "appear" function is useful when your text slide has many points to discuss. This function allows each bullet point to appear individually, in order, one at a time. It helps allow the audience to focus on each point you are making and also prevents them from reading ahead to the next points on the slide.

Finally, overly complex charts are never remembered and are rarely useful in your presentation. How often have we heard a presenter state, "Let me apologize for the following overly complex chart"? The audience is often overwhelmed by such a statement and the slide that follows. If you would need to apologize for a slide, don't use it.

Avoid the "laser moth." This occurs when a speaker inadvertently uses the hand-held laser to continuously circle words and phrases on a written PowerPoint slide. One need not use a laser to point to words on a slide. The audience can read the slides themselves. Lasers are useful in pointing out specific areas in radiographs or pictures but are not necessary to point out words on text slides.

Teachers often ask how many PowerPoint slides should be used for a 40-minute presentation. While there is no correct answer to this, most experts agree that the fewer slides one uses, the better. Perhaps no more than needed to clarify the structure of your talk and enhance its key points is a good rule of thumb. Remember that the purpose of the slides is not to serve as a written manuscript of your presentation. Slides should serve as prompts, both for you and the audience, while you discuss the important key points of your presentation. Memorable presenters do this with examples, stories, and cases and use their slides judiciously, as organizational tools and as illustrations of the key information they are providing.

❖ Top Ten Tips for Talks

Many experienced lecturers advise using an organizing structure to bring the talk together, providing a roadmap showing not only where you are going but where you are now. Cartoons, diagrams, and acronyms all work well in this regard, as do organizers such as "Five Things Internists Need to Know About Diabetes" or "The Seven Most Frequently Asked Questions About Atrial Fibrillation." There even is the beloved Top Ten list. As Dave Letterman and his writers are so aware, lists like these provide an engaging organizational structure with signposts built in along the way. Lecturers can use this to their advantage. Following is a Top Ten list that summarizes the key elements of this chapter, while introducing some further words of wisdom—all designed to make your next talk better than the last.

Tip 10. Meet the Needs of the Audience

The most important thing a speaker can do is to determine what the audience wants to know or needs to know about the topic being presented. Many teachers make the mistake of presenting large amounts of data to an audience, guided by the teacher's interest, not the learner's. The key principle is that a speaker should consider what the audience wants to know or needs to know about the topic being presented.

Tip 9. Understand Your Own Goals for the Presentation

Before they put their presentation together, lecturers should be clear in their own minds about exactly what they hope to accomplish during their presentation. This helps them stay on task. For example, the lecturer might have his or her principal goal as one or more of the following: to educate, motivate, or even entertain those who have gathered to hear the talk. If appropriate, list these in one of the first slides. Notice that the goals of this chapter were listed in the introductory comments. Remember, there is a difference between the subject of the presentation, its title (which should be provocative or catchy), and the purpose (the goals).

Tip 8. Hook Them Early

At the start of a lecture, the audience is probably thinking, "So what? Who cares? What's in it for me?" If the speaker answers those questions for the audience at the beginning of the presentation, she will have "hooked" the audience—they will most likely want to hear more about the topic.

An example of an effective opening for a talk about lecturing might be the following: "If we stay connected over the next 40 minutes, I will make you a promise. I promise that you will learn several tactics and skills to help you make your next presentation better than your last. And why is this important to us as teachers? Because success in teaching very much depends on the way we present ourselves and our information when we speak to our colleagues, our students, our patients, and the public."

Tip 7. Keep It Lean (and Interesting)

Having set the hook with a strong opening statement, you now need to keep that fish on the line. Keep it taut.

You are most likely an expert in the area about which you are presenting. You may be enthusiastic and passionate about every detail of this subject. However, your audience does not want to know, or need to know, everything you know about the topic. Therefore, cut down the information that you present and keep your key messages simple. The 18th-century French author and satirist Voltaire is credited with saying, "The secret of being a bore is to tell everything." This quote certainly applies today in public speaking.

The body of your presentation should emphasize only a limited number of points. People will remember only a few specifics out of a 40-minute presentation, yet many speakers overwhelm their audiences with fact after fact after fact. On the other hand, your audience will be much more likely to remember your stories. That is why case presentations (stories) are so effective at keeping audiences' attention as well as making key teaching points. If you present several cases with teaching points your audience will stay more connected and, therefore, will remember more take-home points.

Tip 6. Finish Strongly

It is very important to have a strong closing. The audience remembers your summary better than any other part of the presentation. Don't blow that opportunity. A statement such as "Oh, this is my final slide, I guess I'm finished" is not a strong closing. You must tell the audience it is coming by stating "In summary" so that you will capture their attention and they will know that what you say next is vitally important. Another tactic often used in closing is to say, "If you only remember three messages from today's presentation, please remember the following...." This may entail returning to the beginning, reviewing again the salient take-home points, decoding a cryptic title, or answering a rhetorical question that was posed at the beginning of the talk. Whatever the device, the ending should be unequivocal. While the lecture should provide food for further thought, there should be no doubt in any of the diners' minds that dessert has been served.

Tip 5. Mind the Clock

There is little more upsetting to an audience than speakers who exceed the allotted time for their presentation. It is difficult for any of us to know exactly how long a presentation will take without practicing it beforehand. Furthermore, the presentation should be practiced out loud at the same pace the speaker will use when delivering the actual presentation. If you simply look at your slides, presenting quietly to yourself, the timing of the presentation will be off. This type of silent rehearsal will take less time than it will when you actually present aloud to an audience. Therefore, it is useful to practice your presentation aloud beforehand.

Tip 4. Concentrate on Delivery

Your delivery will make the difference between a memorable or forgettable presentation. One of the most important things that you can do is arrive at the venue early to ensure that the computer is positioned between you and your audience. This allows you to face the audience while speaking, without turning your back to look at a screen in order to see your slides. Getting there early also allows you to make sure that everything works (such as the computer, slides, and microphone) and understand how everything works so that you are not embarrassed or clumsy while presenting. When speaking, you want to make sure that your pace is appropriate for easy listening. Many speakers simply talk way too fast. The audience can't process words coming at them at a very fast pace and won't stay connected. Remember, when you are listening to a speaker, you are often multitasking and momentarily daydreaming, thinking about other things. As long as the speaker's pace is slow and comfortable, you can stay connected, listen to the speaker, and still occasionally think about other things. However, if the speaker's pace is very fast, it is often impossible to keep up with the information as it rushes past; in the end, the audience simply tunes out. It is important to keep the pace slow and comfortable.

Another key aspect a speaker must remember during the presentation is to use the pause. The pause serves several purposes: It allows the audience to have a momentary break; it allows speakers to think of their next idea and exactly how they wish to phrase it; and it is the antidote for the unprofessional and distracting "ums" and "ahs." Speakers often use these utterances as fillers while trying to think of the next word or thought. The pause (saying nothing for a moment or two) will cure this distracting habit. To a speaker, a short pause seems like an eternity of silence, but to an audience it is simply a brief respite.

Tip 3. Don't Just Talk, Perform
This is one of the most difficult concepts for medical professionals to embrace. By making your presentation a performance, you do not need to wear a costume, tell jokes, or tap dance. However, it is important to use a few techniques that will improve your connection to your audience. One of the most important techniques is simply to smile. Audiences want speakers to be successful, and they want to feel connected. Smiling at appropriate times during your presentation will help accomplish this. It is amazing how often speakers are concentrating so much on the details and facts in their presentation that they are actually frowning, not smiling. This is a turnoff to the audience and makes the speaker appear unapproachable.

Audiences love to hear stories and look at pictures. This is also true for physician audiences. They are interested in stories about you and how you became interested in the topic that you are presenting. Physician audiences especially connect with patient cases or stories.

Another way to connect with the audience is by showing passion and enthusiasm for the topic you are presenting. Few things are more distressing to an audience then a dispassionate speaker with a soft, monotonous voice. The best way to learn how you come across to an audience is to watch a video of one of your presentations. While you may feel anxious just thinking about doing this, we assure you it can be one of the most meaningful learning experiences that you will have.

Remember, audiences will attend your presentation for educational value, but they also want to be entertained. You can entertain with humor, pictures, videos, cases, or sharing of memorable interactions with patients. Bear in mind that your audience attends a presentation for educational value, but it is the connection with you through your smile, enthusiasm, stories, and pictures that will make your presentation memorable to them. Think of this as "edu-tainment."

If humor is part of your personality, don't be afraid to use it during your presentation. If humor is not part of your personality, you don't need to use it. However, if you do use humor, use appropriate humor. One type of effective humor is self-deprecating humor. When teachers make fun of themselves, it connects them to the audience, makes them appear genuine and humble, and helps forge a connection. Occasionally a speaker on stage will tease one of the other speakers or a friend who may be in the audience. This does not always come across well and can make the speaker appear mean-spirited, even though that was never the speaker's intention. Humor should be used with care.

Tip 2. Learn How to Handle Nervousness

Public speaking is one of the greatest fears of human beings. It has been stated, only half jokingly, that at a funeral, most people would rather be in the coffin than forced to deliver the eulogy. Therefore, most of us, if we are honest, admit to feeling nervous before a big presentation. What is important to remember is that most anxiety does not show. Video is quite revealing; watch yourself on video giving a presentation. Most often even those who report feeling nervous come across as far more calm and effective then they would have thought. Almost all novice lecturers who stated that they felt nervous while being videotaped agreed that when they watched the playback, the nervousness did not show. However, sometimes when a person is nervous the parasympathetic nerves take over and the mouth gets dry. This can cause one's voice to crack and interfere with volume and projection. Therefore, it is always reasonable to keep well-hydrated before a presentation and to have a glass of water available at the lectern if needed.

Tip 1. Practice, Practice, Practice

Physicians should take every opportunity they get to do lecture presentations and take the time to practice them beforehand, using the tips offered in this chapter. The more you practice, the better your presentations.

Finally, one of the most helpful things you can do is to get a trusted colleague or mentor to listen to your presentation and provide constructive criticism before the actual delivery. Listening openly to a constructive critique along with watching yourself present on video can be your most valuable learning experiences.

❖ Summary

In summary, the goals for this chapter were to get your buy-in that medical professionals need skills in presentation, to review tips to improve your future presentations, to motivate you to use these skills when creating future presentations, and to improve your ability to constructively critique your own future presentations and those of your colleagues.

If you remember only three things from this chapter, remember to meet the needs of your audience (answer the why, who, and what questions), organize the presentation (an opening hook, limited number of teaching points, and a strong closing), and make it a performance (engage your audience by smiling and showing enthusiasm). By remembering these simple tips, your next presentation will go better than your last!

REFERENCES

1. **Brookfield S.** The Skillful Teacher. San Francisco: Jossey-Bass; 2006:97-114.
2. **Brown G, Manogue M.** AMEE Medical Education Guide No. 22: Refreshing lecturing: a guide for lecturers. Med Teach. 2001;23:231-244.
3. **Collins J.** Education techniques for lifelong learning: giving a PowerPoint presentation: the art of communicating effectively. Radiographics. 2004;24:1185-92.
4. **Collins J, Mullan BF, Holbert JM.** Evaluation of speakers at a National Radiology Continuing Medical Education Course. Med Educ Online. 2002;7:17.
5. **Copeland HL, Longworth DL, Hewson MG, Stoller JK.** Successful lecturing: a prospective study to validate attributes of the effective medical lecture. J Gen Intern Med. 2000;15:366-71.
6. **Gelula MH.** Effective lecture presentation skills. Surg Neurol. 1997;47:201-4.
7. **Harden RM.** Death by PowerPoint—the need for a "fidget index." Med Teach. 2008; 30:833-5.
8. **Reynolds G.** Presentation Zen: Simple Ideas on Presentation Design and Delivery. Berkeley, CA: New Riders; 2007.
9. **St. James D, Spiro H.** Writing and Speaking for Excellence: A Guide for Physicians. Sudbury, MA: Jones & Bartlett; 1996.

4

Facilitating a Small-Group Discussion

Karen Mann, PhD

Paul O'Neill, MBChB, MD, FRCP (London)

S mall-group learning has always been a part of the tradition of learning and teaching internal medicine. Although clinical teachers may not stop to analyze their participation in the different formats of small-group learning, it is firmly embedded in the day-to-day practice of medicine, whether it is the group of learners who are gathered at a patient's bedside, those scheduled for a seminar or a time-tabled teaching session, those present at morning report, or handover rounds. It is clear that the occasions and opportunities for small-group learning are frequent and varied and, importantly, that they arise from the context of learning, the clinical setting. Small-group learning is integral to all stages of the learning of medicine, from the first-year medical student to the practicing physician.

The advantages that small-group learning provides students are well studied and documented, and include the following: opportunities for active learning in which students participate and shape for themselves what is being learned; interaction with and among learners and teachers; collaboration in learning and building shared and individual understanding; and development of skills in learning, communication, social interaction, teamwork, and presentation (1).

There are also advantages for teachers in this setting. For example, Kumagai and colleagues (2) found that preceptors who participated in small-group discussions of psychosocial topics reported that those dis-

---

KEY POINTS

- There are many opportunities for small-group teaching and learning in the clinical setting, both formal and informal, and with all levels of learners.
- Small-group learning allows the clinical teacher to be learner-centered, to understand how learners are progressing, and to facilitate their growth of knowledge and skills, both individually and as a group.
- In small-group discussion and learning, learners can be helped to take responsibility for their own learning, for the work of the group, and for enhancing their peers' learning.
- Effective small-group teaching allows the teacher to assume different roles depending on the teaching context and the learners' needs. In fact, the teacher's role may change even within a single session.
- By discussing their experiences with patients in small groups, learners can learn from their own experience as well as those of their peers. This promotes the integration of what they have learned in the classroom into their learning in the clinical setting; it also allows them to gather a larger number of examples on which to build a rich knowledge base.
- As in all clinical learing, small groups offer a powerful context for teaching though role-modeling; values, attitudes, relationships with patient and colleagues, and ways to think about clinical problems can all be learned effectively in small groups.

---

cussions stimulated personal growth and new interest in teaching and in patient care. This seemed to be related both to reflecting on these issues and through enhanced relationships between students and faculty.

Many different terms are used to describe the role of the teacher in small-group learning, including tutor, guide, mentor, or facilitator. This chapter includes all of these roles but focuses on the teacher's role as a facilitator of learning. Facilitation is a complex activity that requires—like all teaching strategies—a set of approaches, understandings, and skills to achieve its potential in helping small groups learn. The purpose in this chapter is to present and discuss those approaches, understandings, and skills in order to support teachers in using and developing small groups in teaching internal medicine.

This chapter draws on existing literature and evidence, identifying best practice in education. The aim is not to provide an extensive review, analysis, or bibliography of the primary research literature. However, the chapter does incorporate some relevant research that supports the recommended approaches and indicates that the evidence base is growing.

The chapter begins with some general observations about learning in the clinical context. It then presents the common contexts in which small-group teaching can occur in the clinical setting. Following that, some learning principles that apply across several educational contexts are covered. The importance of the teacher's perspectives on teaching and learning and the various approaches that teachers may take are also discussed.

The chapter is built around a series of scenarios, which are based on practical experience with clinical teaching and teachers gained over many years. These are used to focus on some key challenges in facilitating small-group learning and discussion, analysis of these challenges, and suggestions for approaches that the clinical teacher might use in addressing them. The concluding section presents the principles of facilitating small groups that can guide teachers as they develop their skills in this area.

❖ Emerging Perspectives

Learning is now viewed from several different yet complementary perspectives, including internal processes, such as psychological and cognitive activities, and social aspects, such as learning through interactions with others and with the environment. Recent work in this field underscores the importance of the learning context and the benefits of learner-centered approaches (3).

Medical educators have increased their attention to the importance of the context in which learning occurs and to the social and cultural aspects of learning (4, 5); these topics are also discussed in chapters 1 and 2 of *Theory and Practice of Teaching Medicine*, another book in the *Teaching Medicine* series (6). From this perspective, learners are involved in a process of socialization, in developing their professional identity, and in acquiring knowledge and skills. This development occurs through their participation in the work of their professional group or community (that is, a "community of practice") (3, 4, 7). The importance of this viewpoint is that any teaching and learning strategy is integrally related to the context in which it occurs. Once described, this may appear obvious to clinical teachers but is often a hidden factor not fully considered in the planning or analysis of any small-group learning in a clinical setting.

A second major emphasis has been the focus on the learner. Medical educators are increasingly aware of a shift from a teacher-centered toward a more learner-centered approach to teaching (see chapter 3 in *Theory and Practice of Teaching Medicine* [6]). Practically speaking, this means that our role shifts from one focused on our teaching to one that facilitates students' learning. This in no way diminishes the importance of our roles as teachers. Instead, it provides a way to think about teaching strategies that can help to support learners.

Teaching and learning in the clinical context may occur in several different ways. Teaching may be deliberate and planned; for example, the teacher may hold a planned teaching session about a particular illness, or perhaps demonstrate a practical skill. It may also be unplanned and informal, occurring when teachable moments arise, through interactions with different clinical teachers, team members, and patients. Learning may occur also through observation of others in the environment, and of how they do their professional work.

Finally, learning in any context may be explicit, that is, learners are conscious of their learning, or implicit, in which they may be unaware that they have learned. Sometimes these activities may occur simultaneously. For example, consider a group of three students in an ambulatory care clinic with an internist, who might teach them directly about heart failure or show them how to measure the jugular venous pressure. At the same time, the students are probably learning implicitly from the internist's interaction with patients and discussions that are being held with other members of the team.

❖ Contexts of Learning

Learning internal medicine occurs in several different contexts. Table 4-1 presents some of those contexts, along with suggestions for consideration of different purposes and roles of the clinical teacher that may occur in each. In each setting, the teacher may wish to facilitate a small-group discussion with or without prior preparation. The formal and informal weightings used in the table (designated by "+") relate to the apparent structure of the session, not to the amount of learning that occurs.

The complexity of these examples of small-group learning is not simply due to the varying contexts or roles of the clinical teacher. The group membership may also vary. The group of learners may be all at the same level (for example, a group of senior residents) or at mixed levels (for example, a serv-

Table 4-1. Examples of Small-Group Teaching Settings in a Clinical Environment*

Description	Formal	Informal	Learners, n	Role of the Clinical Teacher	Comments
Patient transfer discussions	++	+	2–6	Clinician; encourages learner participation; debriefs learners	Primarily for patient benefit; major learning experience for students because of the informal and hidden messages
Morning report	++	++	12–20	Clinician; resource for learners	Both for patient care and learning
Ward rounds	++	++	2–6	Clinician; encourages learner participation; debriefs learners	Primarily for patient benefit; major learning experience for students because of the informal and hidden messages
Grand rounds	+++	+	10–20	Teacher; clinical expert; limited learner participation	Often highly structured, directed by presenter, but has opportunities for smaller-group learning
Ambulatory care	+	+++	2–4	Clinician; encourages participation; debriefs	Primarily for patient benefit; informal learning, "what comes through the door"
Seminar	++	++	6–14	Facilitator; encourages learner participation; clinical teacher	Often controlled by teacher; good opportunities for group interaction and steering the learning
Procedural service (e.g., endoscopy)	+	+++	2–3	Clinician; encourages learner participation; debriefs	Major focus is on the procedure; learners learn through observation, practice, and feedback
Project presentations	+++	+	4–8	Facilitator; clinical expert	Learners presenting individually or as a group on aspects of clinical care

*The teacher may have a role as an assessor in any of the contexts above. Plus signs relate to the apparent structure of the session, not to the amount of learning that occurs.

ice team). In addition, the group may meet just once, or may have a longer existence or continuity. Finally, in some settings, teachers will find they are facilitating a discussion that involves an interprofessional group or team.

❖ Learning Approaches Important for Small-Group Teaching

Several learning approaches can provide a helpful frame of reference for the teacher in preparing for and leading a small-group discussion. These include active learning, collaborative learning, critical reflection, promoting transfer and application, taking on a variety of roles, and learning through participation. Each is described below.

Active Learning

Learning together in a group enables active learning. Learners work actively with the knowledge, through asking and answering questions, contributing their experience and information, and relating what they are learning to what they are doing in their clinical experience. Through these processes they make increasing connections between what they are learning and what they already know, which is called *elaboration* of their knowledge (8).

Collaborative Learning

Learning collaboratively involves several components and facilitates effective learning (9, 10). Motivation plays an important role because effective collaboration can also increase students' intrinsic interest in a topic. Some studies suggest that haphazard discussion may decrease motivation (10).

Cohesiveness is also important. The tutor can facilitate the development of cohesion to enhance learning and trust among the group members. Collaborative learning also involves a developmental component as the group learns to work effectively together. Finally, collaborative learning offers an excellent opportunity for each individual to extend learning through the contributions of other group members. Students report that learning collaboratively produces the most motivating learning environment (11).

Critical Reflection

Critical reflection can aid learning in several ways. First, reflection can build knowledge. An important aspect of building a rich and usable knowledge base is integrating new into existing knowledge. Increasingly, evidence supports that critical reflection is an effective learning strategy that can promote integration of new information and skills and also promote deep learning (12). Second, reflection is a crucial activity in effective learning from experience. By examining all aspects of an experience, including both the cognitive and the emotional or affective, learners can draw new understandings that can be useful in the future. Reflection can also help learners understand the broader context of medicine. It is especially important in teaching and learning about values, attitudes, and other aspects of professionalism. Reflection is frequently viewed as predominantly an individual strategy; however, small groups offer the opportunity for shared reflection on what has been learned, as well as identification of what remains to be learned (13, 14).

Promoting Transfer and Application

A continuing consideration for clinical teachers is to promote learners' ability to apply their classroom learning in the clinical setting and to apply what they have learned with one patient to the care of another patient or group. Teachers can promote transfer in several ways, including drawing on learners' experience and involving them actively in applying underlying principles across contexts. O'Neill and colleagues (15) found that students elaborated their classroom learning with their clinical experience.

Taking on a Variety of Roles

The role of the small-group facilitator is multifaceted. Several roles have been identified, including acting as the instructor, the devil's advocate, the consultant, the coach, or the neutral chair (16). The role of the facilitator may shift over time with a group or even during a session. The clinical teacher may begin a session exploring with a group their understanding of a particular clinical problem or their reflections on a patient consultation, acting as the coach or mentor. He or she may then go on to provide some framework for how the learners might approach such a clinical problem in the future, as well as some detailed knowledge about therapeutics, shifting to the instructor role. When the facilitator is with a group for a longer period of time, he or she may begin by adopting more of a leadership role; over time, however, the facilitator may adopt a less expert role and serve more as a coach or partner with the learners in developing understanding.

Learning Through Participation

Learning in a small group allows learners to participate through discussion in understanding and acquiring the skills and problem approaches of the discipline of internal medicine. As they participate in small groups, learners can observe the teacher's approaches to problems and try out these approaches in their own thinking and talking. They actually learn both "to talk" and "through talk." Furthermore, in many informal clinical settings they will observe the clinical teacher modeling these approaches, which they can then reflect on as a group as well as individually. Finally, through participating in small groups, learners are observing and shaping deeper values about professional attitudes, relationships with other student and teachers, and attitudes toward patients (17–19).

❖ Teachers' Perspectives on Teaching

Every one of us has values and beliefs about teaching that either explicitly or implicitly influence the way we teach. Those values interact with what we know about teaching both formally and informally, and with our experience as both teachers and learners. Pratt (20) has described a very helpful way of thinking about our orientations toward teaching, called *teaching perspectives*. The five perspectives that Pratt describes are transmission, apprenticeship, developmental, nurturing, and social reform (Table 4-2). Most teachers have one perspective as their dominant view, with one or two subsidiary ones. While most of us will have perspectives that are more dominant than others, each perspective has something to offer in clinical teaching. An individual profile can be obtained from www.teachingperspectives.com.

❖ Six Sample Scenarios: Tips for Handling Challenges in Small-Group Teaching

As already outlined, the clinical teacher will work with small groups of learners in different ways. Following are examples of small-group teaching scenarios in internal medicine, along with suggestions for how to facilitate small-group learning in that type of situation. Table 4-3 sets out the scenarios, the challenges to be addressed, and the learners involved. Some themes appear in more than one scenario.

Scenario 1

You are the attending physician at a small hospital and have been involved in teaching medical students for about 10 years. Overall, you enjoy it, but sometimes you feel that the students tend to be quite passive and come to you expecting to "be taught." However, your evaluations are consistently positive. Next week, you have a new group of four senior students who will be with you for 4 weeks on their ambulatory care internal medicine rotation. You usually meet with the students as a group once weekly for a couple of hours at the end of the clinic. Your usual plan is to select one of

Table 4-2. Summaries of Five Teaching Perspectives

Perspective	Description
Transmission	The teacher has a strong approach to a transferring knowledge, and their view of themselves as a teacher is closely aligned to how well they have mastered the subject they are teaching (i.e., as a clinical expert). It follows that for clinical teaching, their goal is for the learners to have an understanding of the medical condition, which would tally closely with that found in a standard textbook.
Apprenticeship	The teacher is oriented toward conveying the norms of the profession; for a clinical teacher, the emphasis would be on the behaviors expected in clinical practice and the application of knowledge and skills within that context.
Developmental	The teacher is strongly committed to a learner-centered approach. The clinical teacher will aim to get the learner to build on what they know and be able to cope with increasingly complex clinical problems and environments.
Nurturing	This perspective combines both the cognitive and affective domains, with an emphasis on supporting the learner as a person. The clinical teacher will be oriented toward the reactions and feelings of the learner, encouraging them to learn through the creation of a supportive learning environment in which it is all right to make mistakes.
Social reform	The teacher is strongly committed to change within society in addition to the needs of an individual learner. The clinical teacher wants to improve health care and reduce social injustice and will encourage learners to be leaders of change, recognizing where social justice may be strengthened.

Data based on Pratt DD. Five Perspectives on Teaching in Adult Education. Malabar, FL: Krieger; 1998.

the patients that you have seen that morning and go through the patient's history, examination, differential diagnosis, investigation, and management plan with them.

The undergraduate program has changed recently, with a greater emphasis on student-centered learning. You are wondering about several issues:

- *Will these new students still expect you to "teach them," or will they be more active than students were in the past?*

- *Will your teaching plan fit with the new program?*

Table 4-3. Sample Scenarios and Teaching Challenges

Scenario	Teaching Challenges	Learner Group
Scenario 1	Involving learners actively in their learning Being learner-centered Knowing where the students are in the program Teaching using the students' own cases Promoting transfer of knowledge Continuing engagement with learners	Senior medical students
Scenario 2	Teaching with the patient present Establishing session goals Working with a large group of learners Using expert patients Handling critical incidents in teaching Being a role model	Junior medical students
Scenario 3	Balancing the roles of clinical expert and facilitator Facilitating skill development Encouraging critical reflection Working with learners at different levels	Junior and senior residents
Scenario 4	Leading small-group discussions Analyzing group performance and individual contributions Handling group conflict or disharmony	Residents and senior medical students
Scenario 5	Establishing a new small-group purpose Cultivating deeper small-group learning through projects Leading discussion around presentation of projects	Senior medical students
Scenario 6	Teaching in the face of multiple responsibilities	Medical students at all levels

- *How can you involve new students in discussion?*

- *Are there any other ways that you might increase their involvement?*

Scenario 1 reflects a common challenge that teachers will encounter; the questions asked by the teacher are important ones. This is the challenge of promoting active learning. The discussion of this scenario highlights the considerations in promoting active learning, learner-centered teaching, and transfer of learning. The opportunities that arise from continuous engagement with a group of learners are also considered. Many clinical teachers will have an orientation toward and experience with the *transmission perspective* as a teacher; in this scenario, however, incorporating or adopting a *developmental perspective* may also be helpful.

Involving Learners Actively in Their Learning

Some groups may at times appear very passive in their learning; however, involving them as a group in learning that is relevant to them at their level and allowing them to work with the information can actively engage them in learning. In scenario 1, the teacher might consider having a student present a case, raising the questions that concern the group members, and having the group work through the case together, sharing their knowledge and determining what they know and what they still need to learn. The group can be assigned to seek out more information in these areas and then have the opportunity to discuss it again. The teacher has an extremely important role here in guiding discussion, helping to ask the right questions, and providing explanations that will clarify any misunderstandings that learners have.

Processing learners' patient experiences is a critically important learning tool; as Westberg and Jason (13) state, "Unexamined experience is not a reliable textbook." Joint group review of patients multiplies students' learning, and thinking through different patient cases increases their future repertoire of examples. It also allows learners to experience the result of enhanced decisions that can result from group contributions and enables them to facilitate each others' learning. Students can learn that there is something to be learned from every patient and from peers.

Being Learner-Centered

A fundamental educational principle of student-centered learning is the importance of focusing on where the students are and what they need to learn. By starting where they are, the facilitator affords students the opportunity to build on what they already know, both individually and as a group. A second underlying principle in learner-centered teaching is that the students gradually assume responsibility for their own learning, as a part of their professional development. Some important options for making learning more student-centered might include knowing where the students are in the program and teaching by using the students' own cases.

Knowing Where the Students Are in the Program

What have these learners already done, and what will they do as they progress? With this knowledge, the clinical teacher can plan or orient the learners to what they should attend to in this experience. Because learners are often at different stages, it is helpful to know something about where they are individually, in addition to a general knowledge of the program. The attending physician might start by asking the learners to articulate their goals for this experience and what they have done before in the program, collectively and individually. This enables the students to take some responsibility for their own learning toward the goals they have set. It also helps the teacher to support individual learners to seek experiences that will help them to achieve their own goals.

Teaching Using the Students' Own Cases

The idea of using students' own experiences as the basis for teaching is very important. Each student experience offers an opportunity to learn both specific and general knowledge, including the experiences of other group members. By learning more about patients for whom they are caring, students can build up an increasing range of exemplars of their own and from each other that they can use in the future, and from which they can continue to build. Their patients also provide an important context into which to integrate the information, and one that they can recall more readily than general information about a particular condition that is not as linked to any real experience.

Promoting Transfer of Knowledge

Focusing on the students' patients can also help them to apply or transfer their knowledge to other patients they will encounter. One of the most important aspects of developing expertise involves understanding the similarities and differences across patient problems. Asking groups to compare and contrast different patient cases they have seen, for example, different causes for the same presenting signs or symptoms, or different presentations of a similar underlying basic mechanism, will help groups and individuals to build a rich workable accessible knowledge base, as well as a rich array of examples, that can be used in different contexts.

Continuing Engagement With Learners

The opportunity to work with a group over a period of time allows clinical teachers to attend to their development as learners (and their wider growth in terms of teamwork, critical thinking, and problem-solving) and as professionals. It also allows for planning of the kinds of experiences that will present an opportunity to meet their learning objectives.

Continuing engagement also allows the clinical teacher to achieve an equilibrium between covering required content and focusing on areas that groups clearly find difficult. Whatever the teaching situation, teaching always involves decisions, and usually some tensions, about the balance between how much we want our learners to learn and how much they can learn well and use later. This is particularly true in groups, where individual members may be at different stages and understanding. Nevertheless, educators, both in the health professions and more generally, agree that learning fewer concepts well and being able to apply them is more effective and lasting than learning larger amounts of information at a surface level, which is unconnected and therefore not usable knowledge (21).

Scenario 2

You are a specialist in gastroenterology teaching a group of eight third-year medical students a session on inflammatory bowel disease. They have learned the basic abdominal examination but have had limited opportunity to practice this with real patients at the bedside. One of your "special" patients is currently an in-patient with a flare up of her Crohn disease. You have looked after Mrs. L. for the past 7 years, and she is very active in the patient support group.

The session is going well, but one of the students is quite brusque with the patient, who appears to be in some discomfort during the seventh abdominal examination.

Teaching With the Patient Present

Scenario 2 illustrates the considerations and challenges of facilitating a small-group discussion with the patient present. Teaching with the patient present is a common context, and defines teaching at the bedside (22). Here the clinical teacher is being challenged within both the *apprenticeship* and the *nurturing* perspectives. From the former perspective, the teacher is concerned about modeling professional values in always putting patients first, and in developing and maintaining the relationship with the patient (19). From the nurturing perspective, the teacher wants also to create a safe setting in which to explore the learners' approach to the care of this patient. The discussion of this scenario will highlight the considerations in teaching with the patient present, establishing session goals, using expert patients, being a role model, working with many learners, and handling critical incidents in teaching (23).

The students in the preceding scenario are junior or earlier in their learning. This raises several important considerations: What have they already learned? How much can be effectively learned from this experience? How can discussion be facilitated? Further, eight students is a relatively large number to involve actively in learning. It is best to consider these questions in advance.

Establishing Session Goals
Establishing the goals of the session with the students at the beginning of the session is very important. This helps to focus both the teacher and the learners on these goals. One approach is to ask the students to state a goal that they want to achieve. The teacher can then add to the students' goals, suggest new ones, or decide on priorities for the session. The patients' involvement in teaching is important for many reasons. Their role in the session should be discussed with them. It goes without saying that patients should always provide their consent to be involved in teaching.

Working With a Large Group of Learners
In this scenario, the group of students is very large to have at a bedside. To involve all learners adequately, the clinical teacher may wish to divide the students into smaller groups or pairs. For example, pairs of students might each examine a patient, then assemble as a group to debrief on the patients' stories and examination findings. If it is preferable to keep the group together, then involvement and active learning can be encouraged by having each student conduct different parts of the history-taking or examination, with other student members guiding them ("What should she do next?") or giving feedback ("What has he done well? How could he improve?"). In this way, the interaction moves from being between the clinician and eight individual students toward a group exercise in grasping and interpreting the patient's problem.

Being a Role Model
Taking a group of students to the bedside is an opportunity to go beyond facilitating their interaction with the patient, and with each other. It is also an important time to be mindful of the opportunities to model a doctor–patient interaction for students, including the clinical and communication skills that are required for her care. This is a critically important aspect of teaching at the bedside because observing the encounter can help students

to experience the ways in which the doctor–patient relationship may be nurtured, and also allow them to learn such difficult-to-impart concepts as trust and rapport (19, 24).

Using Expert Patients

There is an expanding use of expert patients in teaching. In this scenario, the patient could be included in the planning and conduct of the session, with background support by the clinician acting as a facilitator. The group of learners would not only learn more about inflammatory bowel disease from the patient but also observe the clinician modeling patient-centered care. The session might be enhanced by a subsequent debriefing discussion among the group about their reactions to being taught by a patient.

Handling Critical Situations in Teaching

Providing students with the opportunity to participate in the patient's care, even as in the preceding scenario, through interviewing the patient brings with it the possibility that the learner or patient may get into difficulty and require the teacher's help or intervention. In such cases, it may be necessary to intervene in a range of ways, from redirecting the discussion to stepping in and taking over the interaction. Ideally, the students in the group should be aware of the ways in which the teacher will handle these situations before they go to the bedside or meet the patient. Feeling vulnerable and worried about making an error that could not only harm the patient but also embarrass the learners in front of their peers could contribute to loss of trust in the teacher and the sense of security in the environment. If discussed in advance among the group, these and other ground rules can empower the student to engage more fully. If an incident occurs and the teacher has to intervene, it is important also to discuss the matter as soon after its occurrence as possible. If this is done as a group, then great care is needed so that the debriefing can focus on what can be learned from the situation by all of the participants, not just the learner specifically involved. Learners can also support each other in these situations by helping to explore what other approaches might be helpful in future (13). This type of situation can be common in mixed-level groups as well (including both students and residents), where identifying common learning goals across levels regarding patient care discussions can be useful.

Scenario 3

The junior and senior residents have a daily morning report over breakfast, during which the chief resident organizes a case presentation from one of the other residents. This has been occurring for several years and is well attended, probably in part because break-

fast is provided. The format includes inviting one of the internal medicine specialists from the hospital to discuss the case. You are the associate program director, and so you are concerned not only with the residents but also with how well your chief resident is doing leading the discussion. The patient's case is one of your particular interests—you have published a few papers on the topic from your research fellowship. During the presentation and discussion, you feel that the residents do not understand the finer details of the patient problems and that the chief resident is not leading the discussion at all well. When she turns to you to ask your opinion, you are not sure what to do.

In scenario 3, the clinical teacher may be concerned from the *transmission* perspective as learners at this stage should have correct information. The teacher may also wish to adopt a *developmental* perspective, which would highlight helping learners to think more critically about their learning.

As in scenario 1, a primary concern is to involve the learners actively; however, the challenges here are different. In this particular scenario, new challenges present themselves. First, the learners are at different levels, and are more advanced than in scenario 1. Moreover, at this stage of their learning, the teacher is concerned equally with the amount and depth of their knowledge, as well as their skills at learning. In addition, the teacher is challenged to assist the resident to develop skills so as to gain mastery of the content.

Balancing the Roles of Clinical Expert and Facilitator

Teaching often involves a tension between the teacher's clinical expertise and his or her role of facilitating the learners' ability to grow and acquire new knowledge and skills. The preceding scenario illustrates that sometimes leading a small-group discussion may be best done by coaching from the side rather than leading directly. In this case, the principle of learner-centeredness can guide the teacher's course of action. Asking the presenting resident a question that may help to move him along in the discussion can help model for the chief resident what you consider valuable discussion skills, as well as to demonstrate the level of content mastery expected. Asking questions of the group can similarly demonstrate the depth and use of knowledge. A question that might work for either the resident or the group would be as follows: "Could we stop and summarize what we know and what questions we have still to discuss?"

Facilitating Skill Development

Scenario 3 illustrates that the clinical teacher is often challenged to facilitate different learning goals simultaneously. In this case, the teacher wants to advance both the chief resident's skills in leading the discussion and the acquisition of knowledge by the group. To assist the chief resident, the clinical teacher may wish to meet with her independently of the group to discuss what the goals of the rounds are and the approaches that may be effective in facilitation. Providing feedback to the resident will be an important way to promote skill development, along with repeated opportunities to practice.

Encouraging Critical Reflection
Following the interaction, the teacher might ask the group to reflect on the discussion and how they perceive it went. Most of the points that the teacher might want to raise may be raised by other learners, but once the other learners have made their observations, the teacher can add those that are important to raise with regard to both process and content. However, it is useful to remember that, in some cases, it is appropriate for learners to not come to a full and correct diagnosis during an initial discussion. The teacher's role may be to encourage learners to check on the information they have shared, and may ask some questions that stimulate learners to carry out some further work independently (25).

Working With Learners at Different Levels
Small-group discussions within a clinical context are often complicated by having different levels of learners present, particularly in informal contexts such as ward rounds, where there might be junior medical students through to senior residents. In this scenario, both junior and senior residents are involved. Here, the participants can learn not simply from what is being discussed but also by acting as teacher or facilitator for each other. The role of the clinical teacher may simply be as an expert resource or by ensuring that all learners are stretched through occasional questions or steering. For example, the teacher may want to start with a junior learner, by asking her, "What do you think is going on?" or "What do you think is the patient's main problem today?" Once the learner has had a chance to respond, the teacher might ask a more senior learner to add to what has been said, or to answer any questions. The teacher can model how to manage this without dismissing or belittling the junior learner's input. In addition, explaining how you intend to conduct the session in advance will help to make a safe environment for the learners.

Scenario 4

In your hospital, you established a journal club for residents and senior medical students a few years ago that runs every Friday at lunchtime. Those attending bring along a brown bag lunch; there is a fixed order of rotation for choosing and presenting an article.

You chair the discussion. Over the last few months, the atten-
dance has fallen off, and a couple of residents have withdrawn
from presenting at the last moment. You are not sure whether
there is a problem, although one of your colleagues has men-
tioned that there is some conflict among the residents. Reflecting
on this, you wonder whether one or two of the residents have been
quite vocal in the discussion and have been a bit critical of some
of the female medical students when they were presenting an arti-
cle on HIV. This has never happened before, and you are not sure
how to tackle it.

This scenario presents a common and difficult challenge, that of managing group conflict or disharmony. Several teaching perspectives may be
relevant in this scenario. First, from a *nurturing perspective*, the clinical
teacher may be concerned about the safety of the learning environment,
particularly when the learners are the presenters. Second, the teacher may
have an opportunity to highlight the *social reform perspective*, which is
traditionally difficult to implement. Putting aside the jargon or social
reform terminology, social reform is often of concern to both the teacher
and the learners. In this setting, issues of global health, women, and poverty
might be incorporated into the discussion simply by asking or raising the
question for the group to think about. Third, there is an opportunity for the
teacher to involve the group in analysis of the group's dynamics and in
generating solutions.

Leading Small-Group Discussions
As noted above, facilitating and leading a small group may involve several
different roles and functions of the teacher, including acting as the instructor, the devil's advocate, the consultant, the coach, or the neutral chair.
Which roles and how the teacher selects and assumes them will depend on
the two factors: the goals for the group and the group dynamics. In the
context of the journal club, the goals may vary, although learning in this
setting provides the opportunity for students to acquire new information
and understanding and to develop skills in examining the literature. There
are also opportunities to develop self-directed and lifelong learning skills
and skills in participating in this type of learning. Because these are skills
best learned experientially, through practice and feedback (18), the role of
the leader may be to help to set the framework and standards for the
group's work, and then to gradually fade to take a role of participant and
coach or consultant. In general, groups who are just beginning or who are
working at new tasks may need more direction and guidance; however, the
goal is always that the group gain independence as early as possible. As stu-

dents become more senior, they seem to value the teacher's being more of an educational resource, allowing them to lead the discussion (26).

Westberg and Jason (25) describe the role of the leader as having four aspects: *diagnosing* where the learners are; *modeling* the desired behaviors and thinking processes explicitly; *coaching* the learners and group; and finally *fading*, so that the learners can independently conduct their group. Like many such processes, this cycle is iterative, and as a leader, the teacher may need to regularly return to the process of diagnosing, modeling, et cetera, regularly.

Effective groups have been described by students (16) as including the following elements: effective tutors, positive group atmosphere, active student participation, adherence to the group goals, clinical relevance, and cases that promote thinking and problem-solving.

The literature in this area concurs, describing effective groups as those that build on prior knowledge and experience, have relevance to perceived needs, involve active learning, are focused around problems, involve cycles of action and reflection on learning, and allow for the learning of skills (27).

Westberg and Jason (25) also describe the characteristics of effective groups as follows:

- The group leader is comfortable and has the skills needed.
- There is trust and respect among members.
- The group's size allows everyone to participate.
- The group membership is stable.
- Learners have a common sense of direction and purpose.
- Learners accept ownership for learning and for group process.
- Learners know their roles and responsibilities.
- Learners feel responsible for the group and for each other.
- The group deals with conflict when it arises.
- The group monitors its own progress.
- Group members have fun.

Analyzing Group Performance and Individual Contributions
Leading a small group involves not only analyzing the performance of the group but also of individual members. At an individual level, the clinical teacher needs to be aware of how individuals are participating through answering such questions as:

- Is everyone participating?
- Does everyone have a voice?
- What is affecting whether some participate more than others?
- How do the behaviors of the members affect the group?
- How does the behavior of the clinical teacher affect the group?

Group members can participate in evaluating what is occurring in the group, and the leader can accomplish this by "checking in" with the group regularly. In the journal club example, reflecting with the learner on the goals of the group and how they could be better achieved is one approach. This both helps the group to reflect on its processes and encourages their ownership of the process and of their learning.

Handling Group Conflict or Disharmony

Not uncommonly, as in this scenario, some members of the group may become dominant. If this dynamic continues, participation of other group members may be discouraged. In such situations, the clinical teacher may need to foster more equal participation by directly inviting specific members to give their opinion, or inviting other thoughts (13).

Feedback on group process can occur in the group setting if the clinical teacher is mindful of dynamics and the environment is a safe and respectful one (18). It also may be effective to talk with specific individuals, especially those who appear dominant, disruptive, or very quiet, to understand the reasons for their behavior. These consultations offer the teacher the opportunity to provide constructive feedback and to help individuals consider how they might contribute to more effective group learning.

Among the most difficult and sensitive areas to address are the issues of gender and culture in groups of learners. In addition to the actions above, establishing ground rules about how the group's work will be conducted can set a tone of mutual respect among learners. The teacher can also model appropriate ways to respond and to offer opposing opinions.

Scenario 5

You have a pair of senior medical students attached to your nephrology service for 4-week clerkships. They integrate well with the rest of the team and get involved in morning ward rounds and presenting patients. However, you also think that there is an opportunity for them to use the clerkship to study something in depth. You have asked to meet them early next week to talk about this and to seek their views about doing a mini-project around one of the patients and presenting their findings at the end of the clerkship.

In scenario 5, the involvement of medical students appears to be going well, with a strong sense of *apprenticeship* and participation. However, the teacher also brings an orientation toward a *developmental* perspective with the aim of helping the students reach a new, deeper level of understanding. The challenges and considerations for the teacher include refocusing the group, helping students to achieve more depth, and leading discussions around presentations.

Establishing a New Small-Group Purpose

The first task to be addressed is establishing a new format for small-group interaction; the teacher probably would like to do this explicitly. In this scenario, the teacher has called a meeting to discuss this with the pair of learners, to describe the new approach and its purpose, and to invite their views. By doing so, the teacher encourages a learner-centered approach and early engagement in an active learning process, with the learners having an opportunity to express their needs. The first meeting can embed this approach, through discussion of the ground rules that the students will use in conducting and presenting mini-projects.

Cultivating Deeper Small-Group Learning Through Projects

Projects are often considered an individual pursuit, with the only interaction being at the final, presentation, session. However, they can be used to encourage team working through topics being devised, researched, and presented by pairs (or other multiples) of students. This will often facilitate a much greater degree of interaction between students, including giving feedback. Learners may sometimes view projects and concentrating in depth as conflicting with their need to read widely, yet such projects may help them to see below the surface of their experience and foster deeper connections.

Leading Discussion Around Presentation of Projects

Students sometimes appear to expect the clinical teacher to lead any discussion or presentation, with each member "sitting back" until it is their turn on the stage. When setting the ground rules for the project work, the physician in this scenario can help learners to a clear understanding of the teacher's role as a facilitator and, while their clinical expertise can occasionally be drawn on, learners should lead the work, including presentations. The teacher can play an important role in promoting students' critical reflections on the group projects and their integration of what they have learned with their clinical experience.

Scenario 6

You have received your recent evaluations from the medical students about their clerkship with you. Overall, the evaluation is good, but the same problem keeps recurring—the students highlight the lack of teaching in the morning "sign outs." You appreciate this, but the unit is very busy and you are always pressured for time. It is a real dilemma because you feel that students do tend to be ignored and are "flies on the wall," but you do not know what to do.

Scenario 6 presents a time-honored challenge: teaching in the face of multiple responsibilities and when there is no time. The patient transfer discussions, when patients are signed over to the oncoming team, are an important forum for teaching and learning. While the size of the group may vary, this clinical setting offers an excellent opportunity for learners at all levels to participate in the discussion of patients and problem-solving around all aspects of their care. The challenge presented here is juggling the needs of patients and other responsibilities with the needs of learners. It also challenges the teacher to take a *developmental perspective* to help students think more critically.

To take advantage of this situation involves thinking about ways to actively involve all learners. Some examples include:

- At the start of the discussion, the teacher can invite learners to think with the person next to them about a particular treatment or plan and to commit in their minds to what they think is going on. This involves them actively in working with the facts of the patient's problem. Subsequently, if the resident or more senior learner talks about what has been done or is planned, the other learners can compare their thinking to that presented. The facilitator can add explanation if necessary.

- At some point, the faculty member can identify a general principle that arises from the discussion for at least one of the patients and briefly talk about it. This will encourage engagement, while not disrupting the flow of clinical work. It also helps learners to generalize from their experience to broader concepts.

- At the end of patient transfer discussions, the teacher might describe to the group the most common errors that learners make in cases like those discussed, and explain one (or more if time permits) of those. Distinguished clinical teachers have been shown to carry in their heads "teaching scripts" that include the main features of particular patient problems, and the most common errors that learners make (28) (see chapter 1 in this book).

- The clinical teacher can also facilitate debate as the discussion proceeds by asking questions for all learners to think about, and that can be returned to and built upon, at intervals through group deliberation. This will help the teacher gain insight about the way the learners are thinking and about what knowledge they have.

- Encouraging learners by affirming to the group what they have done well will facilitate participation. This does not imply that the students must have achieved the "right" answer; they may have illustrated that they know or are developing appropriate ways of framing a problem, and that progress could be reinforced.
- Providing feedback to correct errors should be done carefully, and may be done within the group or privately, depending on the internist's judgment. If the goals are for the entire group to learn, then a discussion of how things might be enhanced can best be facilitated within the group (18).

Many readers will recognize these suggestions as being similar to those included as part of the "One-Minute Preceptor" approach to teaching (29); this is also discussed in chapter 5 of *Teaching in Your Office* (30), part of the *Teaching Medicine* series. As shown here, these skills can be used in many situations, especially those where time for teaching is constrained.

❖ General Approaches in Facilitating Small Groups

This chapter has used various challenges that arise frequently in small-group discussion to illustrate some relevant teaching and learning considerations. There are, of course, several recommendations or suggestions that cut across all contexts of small-group teaching and can be applied in different ways. These are summarized below.

Preparing for Small-Group Teaching

The effectiveness of any teaching activity is enhanced by preparation. However, in the clinical setting, the varied and sometimes unpredictable opportunities for teaching can prompt a fresh vision of what preparation entails. Some things the facilitator may consider include:

- The size and mix of the group
- Where these learners are in their curriculum and where the particular teaching fits
- What the purpose of the teaching session will be
- The learners' previous individual experience and level of competence
- Any other resources needed, for example, a patient or a reference.

Some of this information will be known to the teacher, and some may need to be gleaned at the session. For example, a quick survey in the group can reveal what learners' previous experience is, as well as activate what they already know about a topic, thus enhancing their readiness to learn. Pre-paration also includes considering where the teaching will occur: Will there be a room where the group can sit comfortably and talk without concern for their own or patients' confidentiality? It is also useful for the teacher to reflect on his or her previous experience as both a learner and a teacher. What facilitated learning about this topic or in this way for him or her? What has he or she found that works best in his or her teaching experience? Finally, it may be helpful, where possible, to review any resources or materials for the teacher to refresh his or her mind and help to focus on the task and goal.

Leading a Small Group

Creating an effective small group involves both the facilitator and the learners, working toward a shared goal. The leader's primary task is building a learning community. Critical to this goal is to establish a climate where trust and collaboration can be developed and maintained. Introductions at the first meeting are important; a discussion of the goals and expectations for the group and of ground rules for how it will do its work help to involve learners in contributing to the success of the group and developing ownership in the learning that occurs there. For example, the teacher might use the following question: "In your experience, what makes for a group that works well?" The teacher, as leader, can expand on any of the students' statement and add additional ones. The teacher can also talk about what his or her expectations are for the group and for the students. Some groups choose to develop a contract that involves both the teacher and the learners. However they are developed, the leader needs to keep those goals in mind, and to help learners reflect on their progress in relation to them.

Once the group has been formed and the learning sessions begun, the leader's task is to be observant and to monitor not only what is being learned but how. One of the leader's important roles is to reflect back to the group what is happening in both of these areas.

The leader's role is to encourage active participation by all the learners. This can be achieved in several ways: ensuring the relevance of the discussion by relating this to the learners' experience; suggesting resources that may help to enlarge understanding; asking questions rather than making statements; fostering interaction among the members; and observing whether and how all members can participate and have a voice in the discussion.

The leader's role may change in the course of a session or over time. While facilitation may require more direction from the clinical teacher in the earlier stages of its work, the goals should always be to facilitate the group's achieving ownership of and independence in its work. As the learners assume responsibility for the group and for their learning, the facilitator's role may focus more on process. Actions such as reflecting to and with the group on their process, providing feedback to the group progress, and changing the pace of discussion periodically are all part of the monitoring and managing of discussion.

Inevitably, conflict may arise in groups, whether due to different points of view about the topic or means to achieve the group goals, or due to different learner backgrounds. If group conflict remains beneath the surface and unaddressed, there is a risk that learners will become disheartened and disengaged. Regular reflection on how the group is progressing can prevent outright conflict. However, when it does arise, the group needs to address it and to think of ways to resolve it. Common causes of conflict occur when students within the group may have different goals, or prefer to learn at different rates, or when some students dominate the discussion. The teacher can open this up, first of all with a question to the group: "How do you think we are doing as a group?" If the students don't raise the issue, then the teacher can provide his or her observations. These difficulties are raised and discussed in the group so that everyone in the group can be part of developing a solution.

❖ Conclusion

This chapter has attempted to present to clinical teachers the richness and complexity of small-group teaching and learning in the clinical setting. Several key principles and approaches to learning were identified. The chapter also introduced the notion of orientations in teaching and the idea that teachers' actions and behaviors are often driven by underlying assumptions and perspectives on teaching and learning. To connect these principles and approaches to practical examples, six scenarios illustrated a variety of teaching challenges and considerations. The hope is that clinical teachers will consider the principles and approaches presented in these scenarios and think about how they may apply to situations they face as faculty charged with teaching small groups of students and residents. These scenarios may allow teachers to consider alternative approaches in addition to those we have offered. Finally, it is hoped that readers will engage in small-group teaching with the recognition of the many opportunities for effective teaching and learning through small groups, the enjoyment of working closely with learners, and the power of small-group teaching in fostering the growth of the medical trainee.

REFERENCES

1. **Rudland JR.** Learning in small groups. In: Dent JA, Harden RM, eds. A Practical Guide for Medical Teachers. London: Elsevier; 2005:57-65.
2. **Kumagai AK, White CB, Ross PT, Perlman RL, Fantone JC.** The impact of facilitation of small-group discussions of psychosocial topics in medicine on faculty growth and development. Acad Med. 2008;83:976-81.
3. **Kaufman DM, Mann KV.** Teaching and Learning in Medical Education: How Theory Can Inform Practice. Edinburgh, United Kingdom: Association for the Study of Medical Education; 2007.
4. **Lave J, Wenger E.** Situated Learning: Legitimate Peripheral Participation. Cambridge, United Kingdom: Cambridge Univ Pr; 1991.
5. **Bleakley A.** Broadening conceptions of learning in medical education: the message from teamworking. Med Educ. 2006;40:150-7.
6. **Ende J, ed.** Theory and Practice of Teaching Medicine. Philadelphia: ACP Pr; 2010.
7. **Dornan T, Boshuizen H, King N, Scherpbier A.** Experience-based learning: a model linking the processes and outcomes of medical students' workplace learning. Med Educ. 2007;41:84-91.
8. **Coles CR.** Elaborated learning in undergraduate medical education. Med Educ. 1990; 24:14-22.
9. **Dolmans DH, Wolfhagen IH, van der Vleuten CP.** Motivational and cognitive processes influencing tutorial groups. Acad Med. 1998;73:S22-4.
10. **Dolmans DH, Schmidt HG.** What do we know about cognitive and motivational effects of small group tutorials in problem-based learning? Adv Health Sci Educ Theory Pract. 2006;11:321-36.
11. **Willis SC, Jones A, Bundy C, Burdett K, Whitehouse CR, O'Neill PA.** Small-group work and assessment in a PBL curriculum: a qualitative and quantitative evaluation of student perceptions of the process of working in small groups and its assessment. Med Teach. 2002;24:495-501.
12. **Mann K, Gordon J, MacLeod A.** Reflection and reflective practice in health professions education: a systematic review. Adv Health Sci Educ Theory Pract. 2009;14:595-621.
13. **Westberg J, Jason H.** Fostering Reflection and Providing Feedback. Helping Others Learn From Experience. New York: Springer; 2001.
14. **Frankford DM, Patterson MA, Konrad TR.** Transforming practice organizations to foster lifelong learning and commitment to medical professionalism. Acad Med. 2000;75: 708-17.
15. **O'Neill PA, Willis SC, Jones A.** A model of how students link problem-based learning with clinical experience through "elaboration". Acad Med. 2002;77:552-61.
16. **McCrorie P.** Teaching and Leading Small Groups. Edinburgh, United Kingdom: Association for the Study of Medical Education; 2006.
17. **Kenny NP, Mann KV, MacLeod H.** Role modeling in physicians' professional formation: reconsidering an essential but untapped educational strategy. Acad Med. 2003;78: 1203-10.
18. **Branch WT Jr, Paranjape A.** Feedback and reflection: teaching methods for clinical settings. Acad Med. 2002;77:1185-8.
19. **Branch WT Jr.** Viewpoint: teaching respect for patients. Acad Med. 2006;81:463-7.
20. **Pratt DD.** Five Perspectives on Teaching in Adult Education. Malabar, FL: Krieger; 1998.
21. **Briggs J.** Teaching for Quality Learning at University. 2nd ed. Maidenhead, United Kingdom: Society for Research into Higher Education and Open Univ Pr; 2003.

22. **Ramani S.** Twelve tips to improve bedside teaching. Med Teach. 2003;25:112-5.
23. **Ramani S, Leinster S.** AMEE Guide no. 34: Teaching in the clinical environment. Med Teach. 2008;30:347-64.
24. **Weismann PF, Brown WT, Gracey CF, Frankel RM.** Role modeling humanistic behavior: learning bedside manners from experts. Educ Health (Abingdon). 2006;19:404-6.
25. **Westberg J, Jason H.** Fostering Learning in Small Groups. A Practical Guide. New York: Springer; 1996.
26. **MacPherson R, Jones A, Whitehouse CR, O'Neill PA.** Small group learning in the final year of a medical degree: a quantitative and qualitative evaluation. Med Teach. 2001; 23:494-502.
27. **Steinert Y.** Student perceptions of effective small-group teaching. Med Educ. 2004;38: 286-93. small-group teaching
28. **Irby D, Bowen J.** Time-efficient strategies for learning and performance. Clin Teach. 2004;1:23-8.
29. **Neher JO, Gordon KC, Meyer B, Stevens N.** A five-step "microskills" model of clinical teaching. J Am Board Fam Pract. 1992;5:419-24.
30. **Alguire PC, DeWitt DE, Pinsky LE, Ferenchick GS.** Teaching in Your Office: A Guide to Instructing Medical Students and Residents. 2nd ed. Philadelphia: ACP Pr; 2008.

5

How to Design and Conduct Effective Workshops

Yvonne Steinert, PhD

> Workshops, a common educational format for transmitting information and promoting skill acquisition, often fall short of their teaching potential.... In fact, many workshops do not seem like workshops at all; participants are often quiet, passive onlookers; the workshop leader gives a "lecture" to the group; and questions and discussion are frequently absent. (1)

Workshops are generally designed to promote changes in knowledge, attitudes, and skills among health care professionals. Although this educational method is used commonly (2, 3), medical educators may have had little or no training in workshop design, delivery, or evaluation; moreover, some are reluctant to use this method because of a perceived lack of knowledge or expertise (4). The goal of this chapter is to describe several principles and strategies that can be used by medical educators to make workshops more effective—and more enjoyable. Effectiveness subsumes two outcomes: demonstrable learning or skill development and change or improvement in practice (5). Following a brief definition of workshops and a rationale for their use, the steps involved in *designing* and *conducting* workshops for students, residents, and colleagues will be described.

❖ What Is a Workshop?

Workshops have been defined as "a usually brief, intensive educational program for a relatively small group of people in a given field that emphasizes participation in problem solving efforts" (6). Traditionally, this educational method provides learners with an opportunity to exchange information, practice skills, and receive feedback, and when

---

KEY POINTS

- Workshops are a common format for facilitating knowledge acquisition, attitudinal change, and skill development for learners at all levels of the educational continuum.
- Workshops rest on the premise that active participation and involvement are a prerequisite for learning—and that the learner must be attentive and motivated for learning to occur.
- Workshop planning encompasses more than content and involves a series of interlocking steps that include the definition of goals and objectives, the matching of instructional strategies to content and objectives, the evaluation of learning, and the recruitment and preparation of workshop faculty.
- Whereas design principles are fundamental, it is the conduct of the workshop—and the active engagement of the participants—that will define its success.

---

properly designed, is a time- and cost-efficient method of actively involving participants in the learning process (7). Workshops are popular because of their inherent flexibility and promotion of principles of experiential and adult learning (4). They can also be adapted to diverse settings in order to facilitate knowledge acquisition, attitudinal change, or skill development.

❖ Why a Workshop?

Workshops rest on the premise that active participation and involvement are a prerequisite for learning—and that learners must be attentive and motivated for learning to occur (8). In diverse ways, workshops share many of the benefits of interactive lecturing and small-group teaching since they promote active involvement, increased attention and motivation, feedback to the teacher, and increased satisfaction—for the teacher and learner alike. Educational research has shown that students who are actively involved in a learning activity will learn more than students who are passive recipients of knowledge (9, 10). Other studies have demonstrated that increased attention and motivation enhance memory (11, 12). By changing pace and incorporating a variety of techniques that arouse attention, workshops can stimulate interest and help to maintain attention. By encouraging applications to "real-life" situations or focusing on controversial issues, they can motivate learners. In addition to increasing learner involvement, attention, and motivation, workshops also promote a higher level of thinking (12–14). This includes the analysis and synthesis of material, application to other situations, and evaluation of the material presented. Workshops can also facilitate problem-solving and decision-making, communication skills, and "thinking on your feet." This is particularly important in medical education, where the application and use of information are as important as the retention and recall of facts (8). Workshops also keep teachers interested and engaged, a critical component of effective teaching and learning.

❖ What Are the Steps to Designing an Effective Workshop?

It's important to remember that "Workshop planning encompasses more than content. Anything can be written on paper, but learning occurs more effectively with practical experience and the opportunity to share ideas with colleagues" (4).

One of the main ingredients of an effective workshop is thorough planning (1). Box 5-1 outlines a series of steps that can help you to design a workshop. Each step is described briefly below.

Choose Your Topic

Whenever possible, choose a topic that lends itself to a workshop design and try to answer the following questions: Why is this topic important? Does it focus on a training need or gap in the literature? Who will be interested in attending a workshop on this topic? What am I trying to accomplish—and is this possible in the time available? Although workshop topics are often assigned, it is always important to clarify what is expected and whether addressing the proposed topic in a workshop format is appropriate.

Identify Your Target Audience

Once the topic is chosen, try to determine who the participants will be. What is their knowledge of the topic? What is their previous experience with this subject matter? What are their needs and expectations? For example, if you are giving a workshop on "Effective Feedback" to a group of residents, you will want to know about their understanding of feedback, the nature of their experiences in giving and receiving feedback, and what they are hoping to get out of the session. On the other hand, if you are giving a workshop on the same topic to your colleagues, you will want to ask whether your audience consists of newer teachers who are first beginning to think about this concept or experienced faculty who have already been to numerous introductory workshops on the topic and now want to refine

Box 5-1. A Framework for Designing Effective Workshops

▶ Choose your topic.

▶ Identify your target audience.

▶ Conduct a needs assessment.

▶ Define your workshop goals and objectives.

▶ Decide on your time frame.

▶ Define and design your workshop content.

▶ Match your instructional strategies to your content and objectives.

▶ Choose your teaching aids/learning resources.

▶ Develop a workshop program/agenda.

▶ Design the workshop evaluation.

▶ Recruit and prepare workshop faculty.

▶ Fine-tune the workshop plan.

▶ Finalize administrative details.

You may enter this framework at different stages, and not all steps need to be followed in this order. At times, some steps may not apply and others may be repeated more than once.

Adapted from a McGill University Faculty Development Workshop, "Developing Successful Workshops" (4).

their skills. Although it is not always possible to meet your participants before the actual workshop, it is often feasible to obtain relevant and helpful information from other sources (1).

Conduct a Needs Assessment

Effective workshops address participants' needs. Learner needs, patient needs, and societal needs may also help to direct relevant activities (15). In diverse ways, assessing needs is necessary to refine goals, to determine content, to identify preferred learning formats, and to assure relevance. It can also promote early "buy-in" and a relationship with the workshop participants as they start to think about the topic at hand.

An educational need has been defined as the *gap* between the *current* level of knowledge, behavior, or performance and the desired, *optimal* or ideal level (16). Common methods to assess needs include written surveys or questionnaires, interviews or focus groups with key informants (for example, learners, patients, teachers), observations of learners "in action," literature reviews, chart audits, and environmental scans of available programs and resources (17, 18). Nominal group and Delphi techniques (19) can also be considered.

Whenever possible, workshop developers should try to gain information from multiple sources and try to distinguish between "wants" (subjective areas of interest) and "needs" (subjectively or objectively defined gaps). Clearly, individual learners' perceived needs may differ from those expressed by their teachers, patients, or peers. Needs assessments can also help to further translate goals into objectives, which will serve as the basis for program planning and evaluation of outcome. For example, if you plan to conduct a workshop on technical or procedural skills for a group of residents, you may wish to review the literature for suggestions on how this topic can be taught (20). You may also want to survey the residents—and their teachers—to determine perceived strengths and limitations. Moreover, if time permits, you might want to observe your learners' performance. Direct observation can foster early engagement and model a learner-centered approach to education; it can also help to determine the workshop content and which educational strategies would best meet your objectives.

Define Your Workshop Goals and Objectives

Defining your workshop goals and objectives is one of the most important steps in designing a workshop, especially because every decision that you make about your workshop will depend on your objectives. The success of your workshop will also be measured against your objectives (7). Decide what you are trying to achieve and why it is important to do so. For example, do you intend to transmit new information or promote skill acquisition? Are you trying to facilitate attitudinal or behavior change? Workshops are most often designed to promote skill acquisition (21). Determine your goals and objectives carefully, for they will inevitably influence your choice of instructional strategies, the sequence of learning activities, and the method of evaluation (1).

Goals have been defined as broad statements of intent; *objectives* have been defined as statements describing proposed changes in the learner (that is, what the learner is to be like when he or she has successfully completed a learning experience) (22) (see also chapter 2 in this book). Statements describing objectives should begin with the phrase "By the end of the workshop, the learner will be able to: ..." followed by an active verb that demonstrates that learning has taken place. For example, if the learning objective is knowledge, learners might be asked to "list, describe, recall, or debate." If the objective is skill acquisition, they might be asked to "show, demonstrate, or apply." A modification of Bloom's taxonomy of educational objectives, highlighted in Table 5-1 (23), can also be a useful guide in writing objectives. Whenever possible, objectives should be specific, measurable, achievable, realistic, and timely ("SMART"). They should also match the time available. A brief workshop may allow for the introduction of new concepts, sharing of ideas, or initial problem-solving. Attitudinal changes or skill acquisition usually require more time. In summary, the clarification of objectives forms the basis of course planning, helps to articulate the teacher's expectations, gives clear directions to the learner, and allows for evaluation of outcome. As Mager (22) has so aptly stated, "If you're not sure where you're going, you're liable to end up someplace else—and not even know it!"

Decide on Your Time Frame
The ideal duration of a workshop has been debated frequently. Although it is impossible to suggest an appropriate time span for all workshops, it is important that a workshop be designed to enable the achievement of its stated objectives. It should also allow for an appropriate introduction at the outset and a summary at the end. For the purpose of this discussion, a workshop could last anywhere from 2 hours to 2 days—and it could be designed for learners across the continuum of medical education.

Define and Design Your Workshop Content
The final content of the workshop will be influenced by the subject matter, educational goals, and learners' experiences with the topic (1). Content refers to the knowledge, skills, and attitudes that you would like to communicate to participants. The diagram in Figure 5-1, which in some ways resembles a concept map (24), can be used to help you to define your workshop content in relation to your workshop objectives. This figure can also help to structure random thoughts that are often scribbled on a napkin!

In determining your workshop content, remember to provide *relevant* and *practical* information. Although active participation and interaction are essential to an effective workshop, the participants will want to feel that they have learned something. Workshops are meant to promote the acquisition of new knowledge as well as attitudes and skills. Some information should therefore be provided (1), although there is always a danger of "information overload."

Table 5-1. Levels of Educational Objectives

Level	Sample Verbs
Knowledge: Recall information	define list match name recall
Comprehension: Interpret information in own words	classify describe explain identify review
Application: Apply knowledge or generalize to new situations	apply choose demonstrate illustrate solve
Analysis: Break down knowledge into parts and show relationship among the parts	analyze compare contrast criticize differentiate
Synthesis: Bring together parts of knowledge to form a whole and build relationships for new situations	arrange construct create organize synthesize
Evaluation: Make judgments on basis of given criteria	appraise assess evaluate judge predict

Adapted from Bloom BS. Taxonomy of Educational Objectives, Handbook I: The Cognitive Domain. Appendix A, pp 201-207, copyright ©1956, renewed 1984. Adapted with permission of Pearson Education Inc.

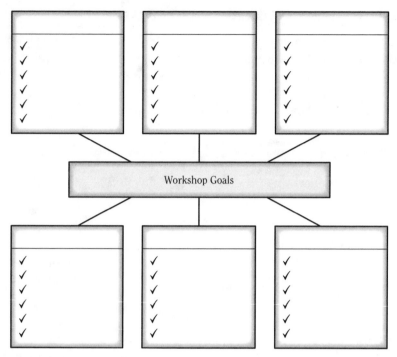

Figure 5-1 Guide to defining and designing workshop content. As a workshop designer, you can use these "boxes" in a variety of ways. For example, each box can describe a different objective (which can be listed in the heading) and then outline the content that matches that objective. Alternatively, all of the boxes can relate to one goal (or objective), and each box can then detail the different aspects of the workshop content (using the heading to emphasize key content). Adapted from a McGill University Faculty Development Workshop, "Developing Successful Workshops."

Match Your Instructional Strategies to Your Content and Objectives

Box 5-2 lists several instructional strategies that are commonly used in workshops. As you will note, most of them promote active participation and interaction (8). Many also enable collective problem-solving and skill acquisition. Try to carefully determine your teaching and learning strategies and to design the appropriate workshop activity (or activities), making sure that your strategies match predetermined objectives.

Interaction is often defined as "a two-way exchange" between the workshop facilitator and the participants; it can also refer to increased discussion among the participants or engagement with the content of the workshop (8). Interaction does not necessarily mean that the participants have to do all of the talking; however, it does imply active involvement and participation by all of the workshop participants so that they cannot remain

Box 5-2. Common Instructional Strategies

► Interactive presentations
► Buzz groups
► Small-group discussions
► Case vignettes and discussions
► Individual or group exercises
► Practice with feedback
► Role plays or simulations
► Standardized patients
► Video and film
► Demonstrations
► Debates and panels

passive in the learning process. Instructional strategies that promote this level of interaction (for example, case discussions, role plays and simulations, live demonstrations) should therefore be carefully considered. These strategies should also be chosen to match the educational objectives, participants' needs and preferences, and available time, and they should promote experiential learning, reflection, feedback, and immediacy of application. Health care professionals, like other adult learners, learn best "by doing," and workshop facilitators should aim to offer a diversity of instructional strategies that will foster active learning.

Interactive Presentations
As stated earlier, presentation of key content is often valued in a workshop setting—to set the stage and to provide needed information. It is essential, however, to keep the presentation of core content brief and to promote interaction whenever possible, using questions, brainstorming techniques, and audience response systems as appropriate (8). Brief presentations followed by questions from the participants work well when the participants know enough about the topic to generate stimulating questions (7). At other times, questions posed by the leader can be useful to guide discussion. Other ways of introducing content in an interactive way include learner presentations, panel discussions, or debates. Prepared media can also be used to deliver information in an interactive and effective manner.

Buzz Groups

Buzz groups can be used effectively in an interactive lecture or as part of the workshop design. Buzz groups are small groups formed to engage the participants to think about the issues being discussed (25, 26). "Buzz" refers to the sound of the participants as they talk with each other in these small groups. By asking participants to reflect on their own experiences and talk about them with someone else, they become involved in the subject matter and learn from one another (15).

To set up a buzz group, a question is usually presented to the larger group. Participants are then asked to work with a partner, or partners, to discuss the question, usually for a brief amount of time. Asking participants to turn to their neighbors avoids spending time moving around the room. The small groups can also be asked to form larger groups to further discuss the same topic or to consider a different approach to the same task (27). When asking participants to report back to the larger group, it is helpful to ask for different ideas from each group so as to avoid a tedious recitation of similar ideas (15).

Small-Group Discussions

Small-group discussions of varying sizes (but typically greater than the size of buzz groups) are commonly used in workshops, especially because they have distinct advantages over large-group presentations in terms of promoting comprehension, application, and problem-solving (28, 29). These small groups can run independently or be facilitator-led. Regardless, however, the goal of the discussion must be clear, as must the task at hand (30). Participants generally value the opportunity to share ideas with colleagues and to learn from peers, and small-group discussions should be built into the workshop design whenever possible. Principles and strategies of leading effective small groups (as outlined in chapter 4) should also be followed.

Case Vignettes and Discussions

A variety of cases can be used effectively to bring relevance to the discussion (21, 31). Indeed, this is probably one of the most common methods used by clinical teachers. The use of cases heightens interest and promotes problem-solving in an effective manner. It also encourages clinical reasoning and makes the learning of medicine "real" (8). During a workshop, participants can be asked to discuss or analyze a case that is presented on paper, on video, or live. For example, in a workshop on "Professionalism," the following case vignettes have been used successfully to determine residents' understanding of the core attributes of professionalism (32).

A senior resident asks a medical student to put in an arterial line. The student has never seen or performed this procedure before.

The resident explains the technique, and then tells the student to proceed.

A long-time patient of yours requests a note from you document-ing a nonexistent illness to recover cancellation penalties from the airlines on a nonrefundable ticket.

An anesthesiologist smells alcohol on the breath of the operating surgeon and believes he is inebriated during a late-evening emergency operation.

Case discussions (or presentations) can be structured in different ways, depending on the stated objectives. For example, a *brief case description* can be used to illustrate a particular point or support certain principles being addressed; it can also be used for participants to hypothesize about what is going on and to problem-solve. Alternatively, residents can be asked to *work through a case*. In this scenario, the teacher might start by giving some information, asking participants for their hypotheses and areas for further inquiry, providing additional information, and slowly working through the case together. Variations of this way of using cases also include cliff-hanger and incident-type cases (33). In *cliff-hanger cases*, learners are asked to read a case that outlines a complex situation and includes a problem calling for decision. The case narrative stops at the decision point, and learners are asked what they would do and why. They also have to defend the factual basis and reasoning that led to their decision. In *incident-type cases*, learners are presented with a short description of a problem situation. If they ask the right questions, they are supplied with more information. As a group, they take the role of the decision-maker trying to sort out the problem. Sometimes they are divided into teams and asked to defend their positions. Often they work alone. The group, however, must come to a decision that is mutually agreeable. The *deteriorating patient* is another type of case vignette and builds on this model (34). This low-fidelity realistic simulation can be used to develop clinical reasoning among learners because it permits repetitive practice with feedback, supports a wide range of clinical situations with varying levels of difficulty, and provides a safe learning environment. The following example (34) illustrates this technique:

You are a first-year house officer. At 2:00 a.m. you are called to see a 65-year-old man reporting epigastric discomfort. He has hypertension and atrial fibrillation, and he was admitted with a diabetic foot ulcer. The electrocardiogram is normal. You prescribe antacids. The discomfort persists, the patient becomes sweaty, and his blood pressure is dropping.

Your supervisor has not returned your call. What would you do next?

When appropriate, *inviting patients* to the workshop can be used to heighten learner interest, and to provide an opportunity to interact with the patient, who might then provide feedback to the group.

Individual or Group Exercises

Individual or group exercises are often built into the workshop design. This might include a reflective exercise (for example, writing about a challenging patient encounter in a workshop on "Communication Skills"), the completion of a self-assessment questionnaire (for example, identifying personal strengths and weaknesses in a workshop on "Leadership"), or the use of a "grid" or framework that enables the application of experience to a predetermined framework (for example, matching cases to attributes in a workshop on "Professionalism"). It is often helpful to allow for individual work before group inquiry, although at times a group exercise is preferable from the outset.

Practice With Feedback

In teaching, as in clinical work, it is important to go beyond the discussion of new ideas. Integration works best by trying things out, and workshop participants should, whenever possible, be encouraged to apply some of the principles and strategies under discussion by participating in a practice session. In fact, this may be one of the most important aspects of workshop design—and should be encouraged whenever possible.

Practice with feedback is the standard method for promoting skill acquisition in a workshop format. The generic form of this method is a brief practice session followed by feedback from the workshop leader or the participants while others in the group observe, learning vicariously through observation and analysis (7). One variation on this theme, which has been dubbed "helping trios," increases the active engagement of the participants. In this scenario, the group may divide into teams of three. For example, in a workshop on "Teaching Skills for Residents," one member of the team may be asked to teach a new skill to the other, while the third observes and gives feedback. A checklist can also be provided to help the observer. After the micro-teaching session, all three give feedback to one another and then switch roles and start again. The value of this process is that each member of the trio learns to appreciate aspects of the interaction that might be invisible to the other—and all are actively engaged. Following principles of effective feedback (35) is also critical in this scenario, as is the encouragement of self-assessment and reflection.

Role Plays or Simulations

Role plays have been defined as dramas in which many participants are asked to portray a particular character, but no lines are learned (29). The individuals involved temporarily adopt a specified role and try to behave in ways characteristic of a person in that role (36), improvising their responses to a particular situation. A role play typically involves two or more people. In medicine, it usually involves a doctor–patient interaction. It can, however, also be used to portray a family interview, a teacher–student exchange, or a multidisciplinary team meeting (37). Role plays differ from the use of standardized patients in that the role of the patient is not uniform. Role plays are generally more flexible and more spontaneous.

Role plays are an effective method to promote skill acquisition. They enable learners to define a problem, to develop solutions to a problem, to try out new behaviors, and to receive feedback (38). Moreover, because role plays generally provoke less anxiety than real-life situations, learners may be able to use newly acquired skills more easily and attend to what is going on in the situation with fewer distractions and concerns. Role plays also afford an excellent opportunity for rehearsing professional behaviors in a relatively safe environment before trying them out in the real world (39). By participating in a role play, learners can discover their own feelings about a particular situation and can gain insight into the patient's presenting problems or life situation. Taking on a different role also helps the learner to experience new feelings and reactions and to develop empathy.

Box 5-3 describes some of the steps that can be helpful in conducting role plays. In brief, it is preferable to script the individuals who will participate in the role play (for example, doctor–patient, teacher–student) and to designate observers. Depending on the situation—and the size of the group—more than one role play can take place simultaneously. Whenever possible, prepared descriptions of the context and critical issues, as well as the perspective of the role the learner will play, should be used to guide the role play, although participants may sometimes want to choose a situation from their own experiences. Ideally, the individuals in the role play should be aware only of their own perspectives, and all should have an opportunity to participate actively. At all times, however, it is essential to allow for time to "debrief" on the experience. Debriefing is an oft-neglected step that is critical in assuring the success of any role play.

Standardized Patients

Standardized patients are actors or volunteers who are trained to simulate the problems patients bring to physicians (40). Standardized patients generally provide a realistic representation of an actual situation, and they are widely used in teaching interviewing skills and conducting performance-

Box 5-3. Guidelines for Conducting Role Plays

1. Set the stage

- ▶ Determine the participants' experiences with role plays.
- ▶ Ensure a group atmosphere conducive to role playing.
- ▶ Review some of the "guidelines" of role playing outlined below.
- ▶ Clarify the goals of the role play.

2. Assign the roles

- ▶ If possible, distribute prepared descriptions of problem and the perspective of the role to each role player.
- ▶ Assign the roles by asking for volunteers or by giving out the roles as "fairly" as possible (e.g., via a deck of cards).
- ▶ Try to involve as many people as possible in the role play. Ask for some participants to take on the role of "observer." Do not give a role to the group facilitator.
- ▶ Give all participants a chance to read their roles. Tell the participants to "make up" what they don't know.
- ▶ Change the players' identities to that of the role they will play. Use nametags to give them a new name.

3. Prepare to conduct the role play

- ▶ Set up the room as needed. Make sure the observers are not part of the role play.
- ▶ Clarify the context of the role play. Make sure everyone knows what is about to happen.
- ▶ Answer any remaining questions about the role play and outline the time frame for the session. Role plays can generally be brief to make their point.

4. Conduct the role play

- ▶ Make the role play as "realistic" as possible.
- ▶ Try not to interrupt the role play while it is running.
- ▶ Allow the participants to "get out of role"—or to say "time out"—if they are stuck or wish to discuss a particular aspect of the interview.

Box 5-3. Guidelines for Conducting Role Plays (continued)

5. Discuss the role play

▶ Discuss the general issues that emerge in the role play. Use the group for this discussion.

▶ Whenever relevant, start the discussion by asking the person in the "hot seat" how he or she thought it went. What went well? What did not go well? What would he or she want to do differently next time?

▶ Ask the other player(s) to stay "in role" and to give feedback from this perspective.

▶ Ask the observers for feedback. Make sure to give the person in the "hot seat" a chance to respond to the feedback.

▶ If pertinent or helpful, run the role play again.

6. "Debrief" the players

▶ Ask each person to tell the group what it was like to play his or her particular role and to take off the "new identity."

▶ Debrief the person in the "hot seat" last. (This is one of the most critical steps in role plays. Do not omit it.)

7. Conclude the role play

▶ Ask the group members what they learned during the role play. Summarize major themes and issues.

▶ Apply the role play to "real-life" clinical or teaching situations.

Adapted with permission from Steinert Y. Twelve tips for using role-plays in clinical teaching. Med Teach. 1993;15:283-91.

based assessments. In teaching situations, standardized patients offer a safe environment in which students can practice clinical skills without the stress of a real patient encounter (41).

Standardized patient scenarios are most often developed from real cases and are modified to protect patient confidentiality; the actors are trained to reliably reproduce the patient's history and, in some cases, physical findings. They are particularly valuable in situations in which participants need to practice or demonstrate working with difficult patients or emotionally charged encounters. Standardized patients can also act as standardized "students" or residents as teachers practice their teaching skills. Experienced actors and volunteers can provide useful feedback to students on their communication and patient-centered skills. Many academic centers have standardized patient programs, which can provide "patients" or "students" for teaching or faculty development activities (15).

Video and Film
Different types of video materials or film may be used to facilitate discussion and reflection. This might include *trigger tapes,* which are designed to promote discussion; *video clips,* which can illustrate a series of ideas or concepts; or *video scenarios,* which portray longer vignettes, usually illustrating a particular doctor–patient encounter or story (15). Trigger tapes and video clips, useful stimuli for discussion, are generally quite brief. They can also evoke a quick response among the participants. Once participants have become engaged in the process of watching a trigger tape or video clip, a discussion of perceptions and reactions should follow.

Video scenarios, or vignettes as they are sometimes called, are generally longer and are designed to portray a situation or tell a story. These are useful for reflection and practice sessions and can help participants to analyze teaching and learning situations. At times, the video scenario can also be used to stimulate a role play, as the participants can role play what they have observed in the video. Alternatively, teachers can use the participants' own video recordings of a clinical encounter for discussion, reflection, and review (42).

Films (such as *The Doctor*) can also be used as a trigger to promote discussion or to stimulate thinking. Most often, the objective is to elicit an emotional as well as a cognitive response in the viewer and to trigger meaningful discussion (33). Film scenarios should usually be brief and present only part of a situation to promote further inquiry or discussion.

Demonstrations
The use of demonstrations as an instructional strategy is often overlooked. However, live examples are invaluable in workshops that are designed to promote skill acquisition. For example, in a workshop on "Teaching Procedural Skills," the demonstration of specific techniques by a colleague or expert can be very helpful, especially if the demonstration is followed by a commentary on what was done well and what might require improvement. Similarly, in a workshop on "Effective Teamwork," the demonstration of team dynamics during sign-out rounds can be extremely informative and beneficial in promoting self-assessment and an understanding of fundamental concepts "in action."

Debates and Panels
Debates promote interaction and the demonstration of knowledge. This potentially lively educational strategy can be conducted in many ways (43, 44). For example, in a workshop on the "Management of Diabetes," the group can be divided in two and learners can be asked to support two different sides of a particular issue. Alternatively, assignment of "sides" can also take place ahead of time, and learners can be asked to prepare their positions on the basis of preassigned readings. Workshop participants can also be asked to seat themselves according to their point of view. The group can then proceed by asking "each side" to state their views. Moreover, although neither side may contain the whole truth, it can be energizing to defend a particular perspective. Learners choosing a middle ground should be invited to defend their reasoning and observers should be asked to vote, so that all feel involved and engaged in the topic at hand (8). Panel discussions can serve a similar purpose, although they usually involve fewer learners and more structure.

Choose Your Teaching Aids/Learning Resources
A variety of teaching aids and learning resources can be used effectively during workshops. However, each must be chosen carefully so that they match the educational goals and objectives.

Written Materials
Written materials assist in the organization of key concepts, promote the retention of information, and remove pressure on the teacher to lecture (8). Written materials can also structure the discussion or promote reflection.

Handouts are commonly used in a workshop to highlight key content, summarize the pertinent literature, or guide the discussion. The literature on handouts suggests that incomplete handouts, such as outlines that are filled in by the participant or are used to organize note-taking, promote greater attention and retention of the material taught (28). For example, in a workshop on "Leadership," handouts may include a summary of models of leadership, the attributes of effective leaders, and common problems in leading professionals. Worksheets can also be used to supplement handouts, as can case vignettes or scenarios. Worksheets are often designed to guide the application of knowledge or reflection on experience and can include conceptual frameworks or predetermined questions to facilitate the task at hand. Case vignettes or scenarios, as discussed in the preceding section, can similarly provoke discussion, reflection, or application of concepts to new situations. Written copies of slides or carefully chosen readings also fall in the category of handouts. For example, copies of slides allow learners to participate more in thinking about the concepts under discussion rather than writing down every word of the lecture (8). Participants may also value additional reading materials that can be used to supplement the workshop materials, and workshop facilitators may choose to distribute key articles, reference lists, or Web-based links for further study.

The timing of when to distribute written materials is frequently debated. It is useful before the workshop if the learner is to come prepared with a fund of knowledge; it is more effective at the outset of the session if the handout is incomplete; and it is most valuable at the end of the workshop if the educational materials contain supplemental information for further reading. Critical to its success, however, is the use of the handout *during* the workshop (8). Teachers should ensure that they refer to a handout (or reading) if it has been preassigned. An easy way to frustrate students across the continuum is to give a lengthy assignment and then not refer to it during the workshop!

In summary, written materials should be well-designed, well-organized, and targeted for specific groups. Often, it is the written material that gives the impression of careful planning (7). Handouts and worksheets can also facilitate retention—it has been said that people remember 20% of what they hear, 30% of what they see, and 50% of what they hear and see (45).

Audiovisual Materials

A detailed discussion on the use of PowerPoint and other audiovisual materials lies outside the scope of this chapter (see chapter 3 in this book for some tips on PowerPoint presentations). However, it is important to remember that certain audiovisual aids facilitate interaction more than others, and regardless of the technique, maintaining eye contact with the audience is key. Workshop facilitators should also remember that flipcharts (46) and whiteboards allow for the recording of themes under discussion as well as the creation of diagrams or content during the session, and they can easily involve learners as scribes or co-facilitators. Multimedia presentations and computer-assisted learning can also promote interactivity.

Develop a Workshop Program/Agenda

Figure 5-2 can be used to sketch out your workshop program. Remember that flexibility is a key ingredient of a successful workshop. As important as it is to plan ahead, it is even more important to be prepared to abandon your prepared agenda (1). Accordingly, it is helpful to build in "flex time" whenever possible. Varying your activities and your style is also beneficial. Make sure that the workshop design flows at a pace that keeps the participants' attention and allows you to move the workshop along while leaving room for the group to slow down or speed up the session as needed (1).

Design the Workshop Evaluation

The need to evaluate educational programs and activities is clear. In fact, the evaluation of workshops is more than an academic exercise, especially because the results can be used in the design, delivery, and marketing of future programs (2).

In preparing to evaluate your workshop, it is helpful to consider the following questions: What is the goal of your evaluation? Is it to be used for program planning or decision-making, for policy formation or academic inquiry? What models of program evaluation will be useful to you, and what are the available data sources (for example, teachers, participants,

Time	Objectives and Content	Instructional Stategies and Aids

Figure 5-2 Designing a workshop program/agenda. Adapted from a McGill University Faculty Development Workshop, "Developing Successful Workshops."

peers)? What methods of evaluation do you want to use (for example, questionnaires, focus groups, objective tests, observations), and what resources will be needed to support the evaluation (for example, institutional support, research grants)? Although a discourse on program evaluation is beyond the scope of this chapter, Kirkpatrick's hierarchy of evaluation outcomes (47) can help to conceptualize and frame workshop evaluations. This hierarchy includes the following:

- Reaction: Participants' views on the learning experience
- Learning: Changes in participants' attitudes, knowledge, or skills
- Behavior: Changes in participants' behavior
- Results: Changes in the organizational system, the patient, or the learner

Different data sources can also be used to evaluate your workshop. For example, to evaluate learning in a workshop on "Procedural Skills," you might observe the residents performing specific skills before and after the workshop. In evaluating a workshop on "Communication Skills," you might ask the learners' patients and teachers to assess their skills according to a predetermined checklist. At other times, a self-assessment questionnaire might be indicated. All activities should be assessed in a meaningful way, and each component requires careful planning and execution to ensure success. At a minimum, a practical and feasible evaluation should include an assessment of utility and relevance, content, teaching and learning methods, and intent to change. Moreover, because evaluation is an integral part of program planning, it should be conceptualized at the beginning of any program. It should also include qualitative and quantitative assessments of learning and behavior change (48). Figure 5-3 provides a sample evaluation form that can be adapted to specific programs and used as a baseline evaluation.

Recruit and Prepare Workshop Faculty

The recruitment and preparation of workshop faculty can be a key ingredient to success. Consider whom you will recruit and how you will prepare them. Some of your colleagues may be involved in both the design and delivery of the workshop; others might join you only as co-facilitators. A "dry run," during which the workshop objectives, content, and process are reviewed and the final plan is confirmed, can be very helpful. Through collective planning and understanding of the workshop rationale, "buy-in" and a sense of ownership are promoted. In addition, both workshop content and process (that is, how the session will be run) should be reviewed. At times, a written handout with suggested guidelines on how to conduct the session can also help to ensure uniformity and success. Immediately after the workshop, a "debriefing" session can be held to highlight what did—and didn't—work, and to plan for the next time. Often, this is a critical step in planning for the future. The discussion can also focus on work-

Please rate the plenary and small-group sessions in terms of how "useful" you found them.

		Not at all useful		Useful		Very useful
		1	2	3	4	5

1. Plenary:
    Comments:

2. Small-Group Practicum I: 1 2 3 4 5
    Comments:

3. Small-Group Practicum II: 1 2 3 4 5
    Comments:

4. Overall, how useful was this workshop to you?   1 2 3 4 5
    Comments:

5. What aspect of this session was most useful to you?
    Comments:

6. What aspect of this session was least useful to you?
    Comments:

7. Would you recommend this workshop to your colleagues?   Yes ☐   No ☐
    Comments:

8. What, if anything, might you do differently following this workshop?

9. Requests for future workshops, courses, or seminars:

10. Additional comments:

Figure 5-3 Sample evaluation form.

shop challenges and group dynamics that were not expected and help to ensure that all of the workshop facilitators are comfortable with the result.

Fine-tune the Workshop Plan

Figure 5-4 summarizes the instructional design cycle. As can be noted, each element in the workshop design influences the element that follows: The goals and objectives affect the choice of content, which affects the choice of instructional strategies and teaching aids, which, in turn, influences what will be evaluated.

Finalize Administrative Details

At times, clinical teachers need to consider the administrative details that will ensure a successful workshop. This might include the choice of venue, creating an appropriate budget, deciding on marketing strategies, and organizing logistics (such as refreshments). At other times, administrative assistants can take care of these essential details.

Obviously, the success of any workshop depends on learners signing up and arriving ready to participate. The decision to participate in an educational activity is not as simple as it might at first appear. It involves the individual's reaction to a particular offering, motivation to develop or enhance a specific skill, availability at the time of the session, and overcoming the psychological barrier of admitting need (49). As educators responsible for the success of your workshops, you must work to overcome reluctance to participate and market your "product" effectively. Continuing education credits, as well as free and flexible programming, can also help to

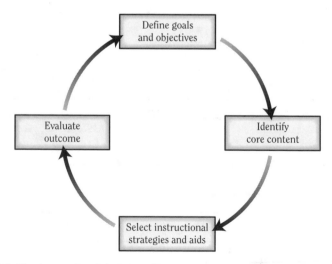

Figure 5-4 The instructional design cycle.

facilitate motivation and attendance. "Buy-in" involves agreement on importance, widespread support, and dedication of time and resources at both the individual and the systems level, and must be considered in the planning of all educational activities.

❖ What Are the Strategies for Conducting Effective Workshops?

Whereas the design principles highlighted in the previous section are essential to the success of a workshop, the following strategies, summarized in Box 5-4, should be considered in the conduct of the workshop.

Introduce the Group Members to You and to Each Other

As the workshop begins, it is essential to determine who is in your audience. If you are working with a small group, it is preferable to go around the room and ask the participants to introduce themselves *briefly* and to state their expectations of the session. (The emphasis on brevity is important, lest these introductions consume an inordinate amount of time.) Introductions also help to establish rapport among the group members. In a larger group, you can ask the participants to introduce themselves by a show of hands. For example, you can ask: "How many of you have been to workshops on this topic before? How many of you have treated patients

---

Box 5-4. Strategies for Conducting Effective Workshops

- ▶ Introduce the group members to you and to each other
- ▶ Outline your goals and objectives for the teaching session
- ▶ Create an appropriate environment for learning
- ▶ Encourage active participation, problem-solving, and skill acquisition
- ▶ Provide relevant and practical information
- ▶ Remember principles of adult learning
- ▶ Vary your activities and your style
- ▶ Promote reflection
- ▶ Summarize your session and request feedback
- ▶ Enjoy yourself—and have fun!

Adapted with permission from Steinert Y. Twelve tips for conducting effective workshops. Med Teach. 1992;14:127-31.

with these symptoms?" Although you may have conducted a needs assessment before the workshop, it is important to repeat this step. Knowledge of the participants will help you to target your material appropriately. Few people like to be patronized, and rarely does anyone want to listen to material that is too sophisticated. Finding out who is in your audience will help you to tailor your presentation to the group's needs and expectations and to minimize resistance to the concepts under discussion (1).

Outline Your Goals and Objectives for the Teaching Session

After the introduction of group members, tell the participants what you hope to accomplish in the available time. Specify what you will and will not do. Preview the schedule of events so that group members will know what to expect, and try to match your objectives to their needs. If you have conducted a needs assessment before the workshop, you may choose to share your results with the group; if you have not already conducted an assessment, consider informally assessing their goals and preferences at the beginning of the workshop. Feedback on the proposed agenda is essential in ensuring consensus between your suggested plan and the participants' needs. As stated earlier, it is also important to be prepared to abandon your prepared agenda (1).

Create an Appropriate Environment for Learning

The introduction of group members to you and to each other helps to develop an atmosphere of mutual cooperation and collaboration. Outlining your workshop objectives and how you plan to achieve them will also help to realize this goal. Effective questioning and active participation by workshop participants at this early stage will further facilitate an atmosphere conducive to teaching and learning (1), as will a discussion of how confidentiality issues will be dealt with. In some situations, participants will be asked to try things that they have not done before. It is imperative to create as safe an environment as possible and to acknowledge the "risk" that the learners will take.

Encourage Active Participation, Problem-Solving, and Skill Acquisition

As stated earlier, active involvement and participation are two of the key ingredients of a workshop. As a result, try to involve the participants in all phases of your session. If you are giving a more formal presentation, invite questions, group discussion, and debate. At all times, encourage the participants to learn from each other. If a problem is presented to the group, allow for group solutions, and consider the different strategies outlined in the previous section (such as buzz groups and small-group exercises) to ensure active engagement in the session. If the focus is skill acquisition, remember to incorporate opportunities for practice and feedback.

Whenever possible, limit group size so that active participation will be feasible. Remember, too, that physical arrangements can facilitate interaction. For example, try to arrange the chairs so that the participants can all see each other. Even if you are working with a large group, asking the participants to sit at round tables can enhance interaction. It is questionable whether you can lead a workshop in a room that is set up in a lecture format.

Provide Relevant and Practical Information

Although active participation and interaction are essential to a successful workshop, the participants must also feel that they have learned something. You can, therefore, also consider providing some information in a mini-lecture format. In fact, a short interactive presentation can help to set the tone, cover the basic content, and ensure a common ground for discussion. Two hours of lecturing in a 2-hour workshop is, however, not acceptable. As well, participants should have an opportunity to respond to the presented information. Questions and comments from the group participants should always be encouraged (1).

Remember Principles of Adult Learning

Adults come to learning situations with a variety of motivations and expectations about teaching goals and methods (1). Moreover, because much of adult learning involves "re-learning" rather than new learning, adults often resent the "student" role. Incentives for adult learning usually come from within the person, and feedback is more important than tests and evaluation (50). It is important, therefore, to respect the group's previous knowledge and experience, motivation to learn, potential resistance to change, and ability to function as co-learners.

Vary Your Activities and Your Style

As stated earlier, make sure that the workshop flows at a pace that keeps the participants' attention. Appropriate pacing implies moving the workshop along while leaving room for the group to slow down or speed up the presentation. Most physicians are accustomed to listening to large chunks of information in a short period, and yet this may not be the best method of teaching or learning in a workshop format (1). Remember, too, that the timing of a workshop is often a challenge because certain types of participation (such as questions and comments) cannot be prescheduled. Make sure that you keep the available time in mind as you enable participants to digress *appropriately*.

Promote Reflection

Recall that reflection is a key ingredient in the process of learning as it helps to shift surface learning of new information into deeper learning and understanding (5). To promote reflection during the workshop, ask participants to self-assess as you go. For example, if you are giving a mini-plenary session on the characteristics of effective leaders during a workshop on "Leadership," ask the participants to identify their own strengths and areas for improvement as you are speaking. If you are conducting a role play on leadership, ask the group members to highlight what they think they did well and where they think they can improve. Feedback from peers can also lead to reflection. If you are reviewing case scenarios on leadership, ask the group to bring in their own experiences and to highlight lessons learned to their own contexts. Clearly, there are many ways to promote reflection in a workshop. The key is to build in appropriate opportunities for self-assessment and contemplation whenever possible.

Summarize Your Session and Request Feedback

As the workshop draws to a close, restate what you have tried to achieve, synthesize the main points made, and discuss plans for follow-up, if appropriate. At times, it is helpful to ask participants to summarize what they have learned during the session and to articulate their next steps (or action plan). In fact, asking them to articulate their "commitment to change" (5), which may include what they intend to do with the knowledge and skills gained during the session, can help to integrate workshop concepts and reinforce learning. It is also valuable to request feedback from the group as to whether you have accomplished your stated objectives and how they would improve the session in the future (1). Although many teaching sessions often end in haste, it is important to take the time to synthesize key points and summarize appropriately.

Enjoy Yourself—and Have Fun!

It is important to enjoy what you are doing. If you are tired of the material you are presenting, you may want to consider temporarily (or even permanently) abandoning your subject. If you do not favor small-group interactions, try another format, but do not call it a workshop. If you are enjoying yourself—and you are passionate about what you are doing—chances are that your participants will have a good time and learn something in the process.

❖ Conclusion

The notion of a workshop originates in the work of craftsmen, as a workshop was first described as "a small establishment where manufacturing or handicrafts are carried on" (6). In many ways, this original concept of a hands-on activity that promotes creativity and results in a final product in a small setting still holds. It is hoped that the principles and strategies offered in this chapter will help to improve the "craft" of teaching.

REFERENCES

1. **Steinert Y.** Twelve tips for conducting effective workshops. Med Teach. 1992;14:127-31.
2. **Steinert Y.** Faculty development in the new millennium: key challenges and future directions. Med Teach. 2000;22:44-50.
3. **Steinert Y, Mann K, Centeno A, Dolmans D, Spencer J, Gelula M, et al.** A systematic review of faculty development initiatives designed to improve teaching effectiveness in medical education: BEME Guide No. 8. Med Teach. 2006;28:497-526.
4. **Steinert Y, Boillat M, Meterissian S, Liben S, McLeod PJ.** Developing successful workshops: a workshop for educators. Med Teach. 2008;30:328-30.
5. **Lockyer J, Ward R, Toews J.** Twelve tips for effective short course design. Med Teach. 2005;27:392-5.
6. **Webster AM.** Webster's New Collegiate Dictionary. Toronto: Thomas Allen and Son; 1977.
7. **Tiberius R, Silver I.** Guidelines for conducting workshops and seminars that actively engage participants. University of Toronto, Department of Psychiatry, 2001. Accessed at www.hsc.wvu.edu/aap/Education/Faculty_Development/teaching-skills/guidelines_for_conducting_workshops_(2001).htm.
8. **Steinert Y, Snell LS.** Interactive lecturing: strategies for increasing participation in large group presentations. Med Teach. 1999;21:37-42.
9. **Feden PD.** About instruction: powerful new strategies worth knowing. Educational Horizons. 1994;73:18-24.
10. **Kraft RG.** Group-inquiry turns passive students active. College Teaching. 1985;33:149-154.
11. **Meyers C, Jones TB.** Promoting Active Learning: Strategies for the Classroom. San Francisco: Jossey-Bass; 1993
12. **Michaelsen LK, Watson W, Cragin JP, Fink LD.** Team learning: a potential solution to the problems of large classes. Exchange: The Organizational Behavior Teaching Journal. 1982;7:13-21.
13. **Lowman J.** Mastering the Techniques of Teaching. San Francisco, Jossey-Bass; 2000.
14. **Ramsden P.** Learning to Teach in Higher Education. London: Routledge; 2003.
15. **Steinert Y, Walsh A.** A Faculty Development Program for Teachers of International Medical Graduates. Ottawa, Ontario, Canada: Association of Faculties of Medicine of Canada; 2006.
16. **Davis DA, Thomson MA, Oxman AD, Haynes RB.** Changing physician performance. A systematic review of the effect of continuing medical education strategies. JAMA. 1995;274:700-5.
17. **Grant J.** Learning needs assessment: assessing the need. BMJ. 2002;324:156-9.
18. **Lockyer J.** Needs assessment: lessons learned. J Contin Educ Health Prof. 1998;18:190-2.

19. **Kelly PK.** Team Decision-Making Techniques. Irvine, CA: Richard Chang Associates; 1994.
20. **McLeod PJ, Steinert Y, Trudel J, Gottesman R.** Seven principles for teaching procedural and technical skills. Acad Med. 2001;76:1080.
21. **Douglas KC, Hosokawa MC, Lawler FH.** A Practical Guide to Clinical Teaching in Medicine. New York: Springer; 1988
22. **Mager RF.** Preparing Instructional Objectives. Belmont, CA; Fearon; 1997.
23. **Bloom BS.** Taxonomy of Educational Objectives, Handbook I: The Cognitive Domain. New York: David McKay; 1956.
24. **Novak JD.** Learning, Creating, and Using Knowledge: Concept Maps as Facilitative Tools in Schools and Corporations. Mahwah, NJ: Lawrence Erlbaum Associates; 1998.
25. **Handfield-Jones R, Nasmith L, Steinert Y, Lawn N.** Creativity in medical education: the use of innovative techniques in clinical teaching. Med Teach. 1993;15:3-10.
26. **Brahm C, Kleiner BH.** Advantages and disadvantages of group decision-making. Team Performance Management. 1996;2:30-6.
27. **Jackson MW, Prosser MT.** Less lecturing, more learning. Studies in Higher Education. 1989;14:55-68.
28. **Butler JA.** Use of teaching methods within the lecture format. Med Teach. 1992;14:11-25.
29. **McKeachie WJ.** Teaching Tips: A Guidebook for the Beginning College Teacher. Boston: Heath and Co.; 1986.
30. **Steinert Y.** Twelve tips for effective small-group teaching in the health professions. Med Teach. 1996;18:203-7.
31. **Christensen CR.** Premises and practices of discussion teaching. In: Christensen CR, et al. Education for Judgment: The Artistry of Discussion Leadership. Boston: Harvard Business School Publishing; 1992:15-34.
32. **Cruess R, Cruess S, Steinert Y.** Teaching Medical Professionalism. New York: Cambridge Univ Pr; 2009.
33. **Segall AJ, Vanderschmidt H, Burglass R, Frostman T.** Systematic Course Design for the Health Fields. New York: J Wiley; 1975.
34. **Wiseman J, Snell L.** The deteriorating patient: a realistic but "low-tech" simulation of emergency decision-making. Clinical Teacher. 2008;5:93-7.
35. **Ende J.** Feedback in clinical medical education. JAMA. 1983;250:777-81.
36. **Whitman N.** Creative Medical Teaching. Salt Lake City, UT: Univ of Utah School of Medicine; 1990.
37. **Steinert Y.** Twelve tips for using role-plays in clinical teaching. Med Teach. 1993;15: 283-91.
38. **Simpson MA.** How to use role-play in medical teaching. Med Teach. 1985;7:75-82.
39. **Cox KR, Ewan CE.** The Medical Teacher. New York: Churchill Livingstone; 1982.
40. **Stillman PL, Regan MB, Philbin M, Haley HL.** Results of a survey on the use of standardized patients to teach and evaluate clinical skills. Acad Med. 1990;65:288-92.
41. **Barrows HS.** An overview of the uses of standardized patients for teaching and evaluating clinical skills. AAMC. Acad Med. 1993;68:443-51; discussion 451-3.
42. **Steinert Y.** Twelve tips for using videotape reviews for feedback on clinical performance. Med Teach. 1993;15:131-9.
43. **Frederick P.** Student involvement: active learning in classes. In: Weimer MG, ed. New Directions for Teaching and Learning—Teaching Large Classes Well. San Francisco: Jossey-Bass; 1987:45-56.
44. **Herbert CP.** Teaching prevention by debate. Fam Med. 1990;22:151-3.
45. **Felder RM, Silverman LK.** Learning and teaching styles. Engineering Education. 1988;78:674–81.

46. **Brandt RC.** Flip Charts: How to Draw Them and How to Use Them. San Diego: University Associates; 1989.
47. **Kirkpatrick DL.** Evaluating Training Programs: The Four Levels. San Francisco: Berrett-Koehler; 2006.
48. **Morrison J.** ABC of learning and teaching in medicine: Evaluation. BMJ. 2003;326:385-7.
49. **Rubeck RF, Witzke DB.** Faculty development: a field of dreams. Acad Med. 1998; 73:S32-7.
50. **Knowles MS.** The Adult Learner: A Neglected Species. Houston: Gulf Publishing; 1990.

6

Helping Physicians Learn and Change Their Practice Performance: Principles for Effective Continuing Medical Education

David Davis, MD, CCFP, FCFP, RCPS(C)(Hon)
Robert D. Fox, EdD

What happened to "CME"? This traditional vehicle for the classic conference, course, or refresher program, complete with the credit certificate for continuing medical education (CME), alas, appears not to have for the most part worked (1, 2). Although useful for disseminating new knowledge and helping physicians engage in well-intended activities, in many ways CME has not contributed optimally to the profession and to patient care.

Why? There are many reasons that CME—at least in its older, passive, teacher-driven, and outcomes-poor guise—fell short of its potential. It failed to attend to the needs of real physicians and was often driven by the content interests and needs of the faculty or commercial interests. It didn't address or simulate real patient problems; instead, it frequently offered updates, knowledge, and research topics on specific clinical disciplines and was often more academic or theoretical than applied. It often offered these updates in settings remote from the clinical practice environment, both logistically and contextually. It didn't help physicians make accurate self-assessments. It didn't present knowledge in a way that could be applied in practice. It rarely considered outcomes beyond attendance. It was not integrated into the practice milieu and was rarely seen as—or sought the role of—a partner in practice improvement or systems improvement. Finally, perhaps as a

KEY POINTS

- CME should be designed to have clinician-learners achieve and maintain an optimal evidence-based practice.
- Previous CME activities have not reached the desired goals of contributing effectively to the profession and to patient care.
- A new construct, CPD—continuous professional development—is needed so that CME appropriately applies to patient care.
- The new CME incorporates the practicing learners' experiences, societal expectations, practice characteristics, and in-context learning using methods that facilitate practice change.
- By fostering meaningful learning, rather than simply "teaching," the CME teacher enables an understood, reflective, and thoughtful application of new knowledge and skills.
- By understanding the broader construct of continuing professional development, the CME teacher can use more tools and methods to impart knowledge to the learner.
- The new CME may not occur in a conference setting at all. It may, in fact, occur in settings and with timing identical to practice settings and be integrated with ongoing clinical activities.
- Effective CME is augmented by tools and resources that CME teachers can provide their learner: checklists, algorithms, and patient education materials are good examples.
- The successful CME teacher recognizes the ongoing nature of continuing professional development, values and uses the learner's experience, and exploits the learners' practice (either the setting or the data generated by it) as a platform for learning and improving patient care.

result of the preceding issues, it was detached from the complexities of clinical practice: knowing what to change, when, why, and how (3).

Over the past two decades, numerous studies of the effectiveness of CME (mostly quantitative, such as that by Marinopoulos and colleagues [4]) and of the process of learning and change (generally qualitative, such as that by Fox and colleagues [5]) have shown that physician learning

requires teaching methods that facilitate learning and improve competence and performance. These improvements would, in turn, increase the
likelihood of better patient care. In short, CME needed a new construct.
Some call this new model "continuing professional development" (CPD);
this chapter often refers to it as the "new CME."

❖ Continuous Professional Development: A New Vision for CME

CPD—or the new CME—includes the forces, activities, and systems of care
that help refine or alter clinical performance to bring about a planned, pur-
poseful change in patients' health. In this new model of CME, the elements
of education and the practice of medicine work together. Both individual
patients and groups of patients benefit from a seamless integration of education, quality improvement methods, principles of teaching and learning,
health care systems, and culture. The goal is to improve physician performance and thus clinical care. The role of teacher is critical to the new CME or
CPD—and to the intent of this chapter. This role must be seen
differently. Instead of simply "teaching," the CME teacher provides an understood, reflective, and thoughtful delivery of new knowledge and skills so that
physicians can apply them and thus improve the system of care—in other
words, the teacher enables participants' learning for the benefit of patients.

Furthermore, because CPD interacts with quality improvement, systems
design, and cultural change, CME teachers working in this environment need
to understand the multiple external forces at work. Thus, in addressing the
entire concept of CME, one must attend to a more thorough learning and
change experience, not just the formal, planned activity that most call "CME."

There are three notable differences between the new and old con-
structs of CME (6). First, CPD is less focused on the faculty and the delivery
of educational content. Instead, it is more focused on the needs, wants, and
clinical care issues generated by the physician-learner. Second, CPD is
more ubiquitous than the CME that limits its location (at least in most professionals' minds) to the lecture hall or conference room. This shift
acknowledges that real learning and change occur everywhere—from a
physician's home study to her office or clinical practice setting to more formal learning environments. Third, the content of CPD is less specifically
factual knowledge about disease states and more broadly constructed to
address the integration and application of that learning. This broader picture
derives in part from the Accreditation Council for Graduate Medical
Education (ACGME) competencies (7), which focus on communication
skills, professionalism, teamwork, and other dimensions of care. Others
describe this shift as moving clinical content from the theoretical or more

abstract to the practical, and moving the educational methods from the didactic lecture or textbook to more interactive, engaging, and practice-based experience. The following case example illustrates the new and older versions of CME, as does Table 6-1.

Learning About End-of-Life Care

Traditionally, the clinician who wanted to learn more about end-of-life (or palliative) care would attend one or more conferences on the subject, including lectures, and read the take-home syllabus or other printed materials. The content of such traditional learning would include explicit knowledge—the dosage of medications in pain and symptom management, for example.

In contrast, newer ideas about CME or CPD entail a broader learning experience that involves undertaking a more objective needs assessment (reviewing charts of several terminally ill patients, for example); reflecting on one or more past clinical cases (asking "Was my patient's pain really well controlled?"); participating in several methods of learning (conferences, small

Table 6-1. CME Versus CPD

Characteristic	"Old CME"	CPD (the "New CME")
Educational format	Didactic, formal	Interactive, engaging the learner, often using case scenarios
Setting	Lecture or conference center	Practice settings, online, and other information technology–mediated methods, plus more traditional educational venues
Basis	Frequently teacher-driven	Based on real and perceived learner needs, patient demands and expectations
Content	Discipline-specific knowledge	Clinical knowledge, plus elements of professionalism, communication skills, knowledge management, teamwork
Outcomes	Attendance	Increased competency, better performance in the work setting, improved health care outcomes

CME = continuing medical education; CPD = continuing professional development.

groups, consultation with a palliative care specialist, on-line self-study modules, and other methods); learning and practicing so as to gain practical knowledge; and absorbing a broader range of knowledge beyond the traditionally "clinical" or disease-based (for example, communicating bad news to families, collaborating with team members, or even appreciating the roles of music or art therapy); and, finally, assessing his or her progress by further reflection, chart audit, or other means to improve and integrate quality of care for the terminally ill.

❖ Teaching in the CME Environment

Understanding Learning

To help explain what is meant by "learning" in the clinical context, the work of Fox and colleagues offers a way in which to understand internal and external factors, educational resources, and the importance of the teacher (4). The authors asked the following questions of more than 300 North American physicians: "What did you change last in your practice? What caused that change? What resources did you use in order to make the change?" The results provide answers that may help the CME teacher or organizer prepare for this audience.

First, physicians undertaking any change to their practice revealed that they had an image of what that change was going to look like—a surgeon envisioned full competency in a laparoscopic technique, for example. Second, the forces for change were widespread. While some drew from educational and CME experiences, many more were intrapersonal (for example, a recent personal experience), or external, resulting from changing demographics (aging patients, ethno-cultural shifts in patient populations) or regulatory and other changes. This first deep study of why and how physicians learn and change, along with many subsequent examinations of learning in practitioners, also identified voluntary self-directed learning actions taken by clinicians once they have begun to try to solve patient problems and address clinical performance needs.

In addition to the rich information it provided on the learning and change experience, this study offers a structure by which internal and external factors relevant to the learner-clinician may be incorporated into CME. Here, given the highly voluntary nature of CPD, internal factors—such as personal experience, beliefs, learning style, and preferences—assume even greater importance than is the case for medical students or residents. External factors also influence this learning. These range from the immediate and proximal (for example, the clinical team and availability of point-of-care educational resources) to those that are more remote (such as regulatory and societal factors). Furthermore, Fox and colleagues' study described the use of a wide variety of learning resources—colleagues, written materials, patient experiences, and team members—well beyond the traditional "old" venues of CME.

Understanding the Learner

In CME, perhaps even more than other forms of medical education, planners need to be attuned to the learning needs of their students. "Who's the target audience?" is a favorite planning phrase of many adult educators, as well it should be. The answer is not straightforward, and may inform an important step in the process of providing CPD. This section briefly explores factors within the learner that impede or support learning and translates the relevant literature into messages that are meaningful to clinicians and their learning experience.

In addition to commonly described characteristics of the adult learner (8)—such as age, sex, training, experience, and learning style—there are subtle but important differences within groups of physicians (for example, generalists compared with specialists). Several characteristics, shaped by their practices and perhaps their own personalities, are notable among generalist populations: their wide scope of knowledge, their need to deal with ambiguity and vague illness presentations, and their need to balance and manage multiple comorbid conditions. The need to understand and address the complexity of interactions in a patient with obesity, diabetes, osteoarthritis, and depression is not uncommon. In contrast, more highly specialized internists who articulate a need to keep abreast of latest findings in a narrower (but deeper) field express comfort with definitive answers to clinical problems (9, 10).

There are other differences, too, relating to the awareness and application of new findings. Some learners may not be aware of an innovation or new findings. Some may be aware of a new finding but have not made the change because they disagree with it or are uncertain about it. Others have made the change but implement it sporadically. Finally, others may have integrated the new finding completely into their practice (11). Each of these learners requires a different educational approach.

External Factors

Societal, Government, and Regulatory Factors

Many external factors drive the learning needs of CME learners, and rightfully should determine CME, or CPD, content. Arguably, of all the external factors affecting learning in future decades, none may be more dramatic or more powerful than the issues related to health care reform. Included in its wide-ranging directions are at least two elements of relevance to CME: the increasing use of quality measures in payment systems (12) and the concept of the medical home (13). Quality measures are indicators of performance derived from evidence, with consensus used to assess practitioners' clinical actions. These measures are increasingly related to funding (for example, the physician quality reporting initiative of the Centers for Medicare & Medicaid Services [14]). Frequently used within hospital and health care systems, such measures can be easily transformed into learning objectives. Likewise, several of the criteria used to distinguish a medical practice as a "medical home" (13), such as performance in patient care coordination, prevention, screening, long-term care management, and health maintenance, all topics of importance in the new world of CME.

More Proximal Factors
In addition to the broad and overarching elements of societal or government health care changes are numerous, more proximal regulatory factors that apply to practicing physicians and other health care providers, and the environment in which they learn. For physicians, state medical boards generally require a finite number of hours (often called credits) to maintain licenses (15); in this process, some states (for example, California [16]) require regular training in specific topics, such as cultural competence. At another level of regulation, specialty boards are moving incrementally away from counting hours of CME participation to "maintenance of certification" programs (17), stressing knowledge-based examinations, participation in a practice-based performance improvement program, maintenance of licensure, and other standards of the profession in addition to traditional CME credits. The American Board of Internal Medicine (18) provides a robust working and evolving example of these changes. Two educational accreditation programs have added to this shift in emphasis, urging more uptake of the new CME. The ACGME (7), for example, stresses practice-based learning and improvement—detecting performance gaps and correcting them by educational and other means. In addition, the Accreditation Council for Continuing Medical Education (19) has prompted CME providers to demonstrate the effect of their educational programs on physician competence or performance and on health care reforms, further shifting CME toward newer models.

Immediate Clinical Environment: Workplace Learning
The CME teacher must also remember the workplace or clinical setting in which learning becomes translated into clinical practice and where its

impact may be best judged. Several issues concerning the workplace are important. First, it is necessary to understand and incorporate the concept of constructivism, in which abstract knowledge is constructed (20). This construction of knowledge, from a theoretical, disease-based approach to a more practical, patient-centered focus, enables its application in the practice setting. For example, knowledge that the p450 pathway is used for metabolism of statins, for example, can be translated into suggestions for clinical practice—for example, asking patients about their diet and checking for consumption of foods, such as grapefruit, that also use the pathway and interfere with drug absorption.

A second factor in the immediate work setting is that of the clinical team—a highly variable instance of communities of practice (see chapter 4 in this book and chapter 1 in another book in the *Teaching Medicine* series, *Theory and Practice of Teaching Medicine* [21]) described by Wenger (22) that represents interprofessional collaboration and education and team training (23). These concepts too are highly important for clinicians' learning, and they frequently act as either impediments to or facilitators of learning. The third factor relates to the clinician's (and the CME teacher's) learning resources: To the extent that these resources are immediately available in the workplace, they may be considered important variables in the learning process. Finally, any discussion of the workplace environment, and the CME that pertains to it, fails if the patient is not mentioned as a key, central, driving element in the process of learning and change.

Learning Resources in the Environment
Apart from team members, patient interactions, local rounds, and other educational resources, today's workplace environment contains many other resources. Many of these have been based on the concept of evidence-based medicine (EBM) (24, 25), a construct that has significantly altered the practice of medicine and our understanding of the word "evidence." These include clinical practice guidelines and online point-of-care reference sources such as UptoDate (26), MD Consult (27), Clin-eguide (28), and WebMD (29) (see chapter 5 in *Theory and Practice of Teaching Medicine* [21]). Despite the impressive uptake of EBM in teaching, research, education, and clinical practice, there are significant problems with evidence as it is presented and available in the clinical setting (Box 6-1). These relate to the degree to which clinical guidelines in particular fail to 1) be integrated into health systems, 2) provide information on costs or quality measures, and 3) be integrated into the culture of physician practice. Each of these "failures" provides an opportunity for the new CME teacher. For example, using specific guideline recommendations as learning objectives, the teacher can build cases for discussion or offer protocols or algorithms for take-home use.

Box 6-1. The "Failure" of Clinical Practice Guidelines (From a CME Perspective)

► Straus and Haynes (33) offer clues as to why clinical practice guidelines may lack traction in the clinical setting. Large volumes of personal experience and primary studies form a large part of the information sources clinicians use in decision-making, followed in decreasing amounts by systematic reviews and by guidelines themselves. Straus and Haynes argue that a much smaller but important portion is often lacking: the creation of tools (patient education materials, reminders at the point of care, and other measures) that could embed knowledge into the practice setting.

► Although clinical practice guidelines attempt to increasingly represent best evidence, their frequent inattention to cost, patient choice, and use of quality measures derived from the guideline remains problematic.

► EBM has failed to percolate perfectly into the culture of physicians, who regard it as teaching "cookbook" medicine that too narrowly defines and limits clinical practice. Despite the increasing emphasis on information technology–based point-of-care learning activities, important internal personal characteristics must be weighed here, too (e.g., the degree to which clinicians actively seek knowledge and possess knowledge management or critical appraisal skills).

Facilitating Learning

The clinician's rich, interactive internal and external environment creates a medium in which learning and change may or may not occur. Different in subtle and not-so-subtle ways from undergraduate or graduate education, the critical role of the CME teacher includes teaching in ways already described in earlier chapters of this book. The CME teacher must understand the setting in which learning is applied, including the nature, needs, motivation, and environment of the learner. The following section outlines the process of learning in CPD, from the determination of learner needs to the tools or methods of CME to the characteristics of the successful CME teacher. An educational scenario accompanies each component of this section.

The CME Teacher: Part I

Dr. Rodriguez, an internist with a sizable academic, clinical, and research-intense HIV-AIDS practice, has taught in her medical school's annual general internist refresher program aimed at community-based general internists for several years. She has regularly filled a 90-minute lecture time slot in these programs and has been reasonably happy with her course evaluations, which demonstrate that she communicates her content area very well. This content has been described as an "update in HIV-AIDS" and focuses on the antiretroviral agents, side effect profiles, and new research findings in the field, with implications for practice. She is puzzled, however; her referrals from community-based internists show a common pattern: problems with drug resistance, poor patient adherence, patient unhappiness with side effects, and a general lack of compliance with clinical practice guidelines. She decides to do something different this year.

The Physician as an Active Learner-Practitioner: The Process of CPD
Successful education should reflect the basic principles of adult learning. In their decisions about how to facilitate learning, teachers and program planners must account for differences in how practitioners learn. Differences between principles for teaching children and those for facilitating learning in adults are a matter of degree. However, among fully certified practicing physicians who are responsible for their patients, these differences are most clearly evident and most important as conditions for learning and changing practices.

First and foremost, the practicing physician most often learns in connection with an immediate and consequence-laden problem in patients for whom they are responsible, even in a team setting. This means that CPD is a problem-solving strategy for these clinicians, and the problems it solves are patient problems. Therefore, education must be relevant, pointed to the problem, and timely. Teachers must use clinical problems as organizing frameworks if they expect to penetrate the learner's clinical practice. To do otherwise is to risk missing the point of learning for these physicians: "Help me solve my real problems."

Determining Learning Needs
Second, because learning is generated from practice, teaching must focus on the perceived and real needs of the clinician. Here, needs are defined as gaps between what is (current practice) and what ought to be (a clear recommendation in a clinical practice guideline, for example). When a perform-

ance or a systems gap occurs because the level of knowledge and skill is not what it ought to be, we have a learning need. In any of these instances, helping the clinician meet that need is the role of the CPD process; in this case, assessment forms a basis for educational decision-making.

Here the new CME teacher can provide a format in which alternative explanations and management strategies can be used. This can occur in traditional CME settings by encouraging participants to discuss (perhaps in pairs or small groups) perplexing patient problems. The same gap-based approach can be used to describe system problems in health care. In this vignette, an examination of several referrals might reveal where the gaps occur—what common, repeated patient problems or other patient care needs are present.

What about clinicians' self-assessment of learning needs? What if clinicians incorrectly perceive what they know and can do? In this case, physicians may think they can do something that they cannot do, or they may inaccurately self-assess their knowledge and skill. These phenomena can profoundly affect clinicians' motivation to learn and change. When they do not perceive these needs, physicians may not feel uncomfortable with the gaps in health performance or in knowledge and skill; as a result, they may not be motivated to address those needs. Consequently, a CME teacher working with practitioners will have little success if he or she attempts to address real needs without attending to the important role that perception and motivation play in the outcomes. If the learner-physician's processes of self-assessment and subsequent motivation are not activated, education suffers because the physician may think, "That's not my problem." The learners may be unaware of their needs; until these needs become evident, the learners will not learn and change. Here, the CME teacher may draw on external observations, such as chart audit, referral data, medication reconciliation lists, and other external data sources to demonstrate unperceived needs to clinicians. Of sizable help in this area, the increasing use of quality measures by health care systems and insuring bodies, and of other objective, practice-based data generated in specialty board recertification processes, can help physicians more clearly understand their learning needs and practice gaps.

Tailoring Learning to the Learner
With the teaching techniques and methods described elsewhere in this book as a guide, teachers can adapt their approaches to meeting their learners' needs. The continuation of the vignette illustrates how these institutional decisions can be made.

The CME Teacher: Part II

On the advice of her dean for CME and an adult educator based in the medical school, Dr. Rodriguez chooses a several-pronged approach to improving her teaching. First, she asks that the CME office e-mail a questionnaire to registrants at an upcoming CME event. In it, she asks community-based physicians to describe clinical HIV-AIDS problems that plague them and their patients. Second, she and an interested resident undertake a chart review of their own records and those of 10 recent referrals as part of a graduate education quality project. Using these data sources subjectively and objectively to obtain information, she undertakes a new approach to her 90-minute time slot.

She uses a handout to communicate much of the "update" portion of her previous talks, and so keeps the didactic portion of her presentation to a minimum. Consistent with the principles of adult education, which value the learner's experience and prior knowledge, she presents several cases for group discussion based on the physicians' stated problems and those determined by chart audit. She encourages discussion in small groups, then solicits solutions from the audience using an audience response system. In this way, she provides a smooth transition from theoretical to practical knowledge. Finally, she offers several take-home "practice-enablers," including patient education materials; communication tips for asking about medication adherence; and a flow chart for use by community-based internists and their staff to monitor medication use, side effects and adherence, patient concerns, and laboratory profiles. On the basis of the clinical practice guidelines, these protocols should improve adherence to standardized and effective management and therapeutic regimes.

After her presentation, she is pleased to see that her post-course evaluations have improved, and—more important—her referrals now reflect a better understanding of and adherence to treatment protocols and patient concerns.

When Teaching Is Not Enough: Moving From the Classroom to the Practice Setting
What happens when physicians do not attend CME activities? Much of the content and construct of CME can be handled in the traditional teaching venues described here as the classroom. However, many other methods, roughly characterized as "implementation strategies" (30), can deliver information

and help transfer research findings and clinical practice guidelines into practice. Returning to our vignette, Dr. Rodriguez may decide that she wishes to reach out to regional physicians who do not participate in CME activities, to those who work in hospital or clinic settings, and to others—even patients— in order to improve the quality of HIV-AIDS care. Several alternative funding sources exist for such activities: State, disease-specific, and other funding agencies increasingly recognize the merit of such efforts.

Derived from a coupling of educational and health services literature, often called "knowledge translation" (31), these measures can include outreach methods, practice-based initiatives, and alternative educational strategies (Box 6-2).

Characteristics of the Effective Clinical Teacher/Facilitator

This scenario and its learning implications highlight the characteristics of the CME teacher or facilitator of CPD. A successful teacher of practicing

---

Box 6-2. Alternative Educational Strategies

► Academic detailing: Visits to physicians by health professionals, such as pharmacists or nurses, to raise issues of prescribing, disease prevention, and screening (32)

► Opinion-leader and train-the-trainer methods: Opinion leaders are community-based clinicians who are considered educationally influential by their peers; the trainer programs frequently use opinion leaders to disseminate information (30, 32)

► Reminders at the point of care: Electronic or paper reminders used at the point of care (30)

► Audit and feedback: The use of data derived form charts, utilization reviews, or other databases to demonstrate how clinicians perform in specific areas and to provide educational feedback (32).

► Problem-based small groups (32): Groups of eight to 10 physicians or other health professionals involved in case discussion and problem-solving.

Data obtained from Dixon J. Evaluation criteria in studies of continuing education in the health professions: a critical review and a suggested strategy. Eval Health Prof. 1978;1:47-65.

physicians can organize content and select methods of teaching that bring real needs to the surface as they address them. This teacher can motivate learners by making them reflect effectively on their practices, clinical performance, health care systems, and level of knowledge and skill in a way that makes learners aware of their real needs. By maintaining a clinical problem focus (mentioned earlier), this reflection is important for practicing physicians because their learning and subsequent changes are mostly voluntary. They must become convinced of their needs and their patient's needs before they will give up practices that they have become comfortable with. Overcoming inertia—dropping a familiar practice management routine, for example—is a difficult process. The merit of such changes must be shown to physicians before they occur.

❖ Putting It All Together

This section summarizes in stepwise fashion the activities of the successful CME teacher or CPD facilitator. It also outlines a process by which to evaluate successful teaching in this area and acknowledges the barriers to implementing this idealized view of CPD. Finally, it summarizes teaching tips for the new CME teacher.

A Planning Guide

Phase 1: Needs Assessment; Pre-Education Activities
Before embarking on a CME activity, the new CME/CPD facilitator begins to answer most if not all of the following questions: Who are the physicians or other health professionals who make up the audience? What have been their training, background, work settings, regulatory experience, and other expectations? What are their self-identified learning needs? What other needs might exist—based on literature reviews or other data sources? How can I best address these needs, expectations, and objectives?

The successful teacher then begins to craft an educational experience to address these specific learning needs, paying close attention to the flow of content, the overall curriculum, and the use of educational methods and resources. Most important, the successful CME teacher has an idea of what the practitioner will be able to do as a result of the CME activity.

Phase 2: The Educational Activity
In the encounter itself—such as a large-group lecture or workshop small-group activity—the successful clinician-teacher will address issues important to the learner, not just the teacher. These are called the three Fs:

- *Format*: To augment, if not entirely replace, the didactic lecture, the successful CME teacher will consider alternative methods, such as case materials, discussion groups, presentation of audit findings, simulations, audio- or videotaping, and other educational techniques. Chapter 5 of this book provides several suggestions for how this may be accomplished in a workshop format.
- *Facilitation*: The teacher will focus less on communicating innovations or new treatment modes. Instead, the teacher will facilitate learning by engaging participants in interactive discussion (with others or experts), problem-solving exercises, audience responses systems, and other techniques. These efforts move learners from explicit understandings of new knowledge to more tacit, practical, and applied knowledge.
- *Follow-up*: Recognizing that a one-time event or activity may be insufficient to change practice behaviors, the successful CME teacher may provide handouts, such as protocols or patient education materials; encourage further dialogues or case discussion by e-mail or other means; or send reminders or postcourse questionnaires to highlight specific points of learning. Finally, other CPD activities not covered in this chapter, such as reminders at the point of care and Internet-mediated learning, can extend the learning experience beyond the "classroom" setting.

Phase 3: Evaluating the Outcome of CME Activities
Many methods can be used to assess the impact of CME activity. Characterized by Dixon (32), they consist of four simple levels: 1) participants' perception of the activity as detected by postcourse questionnaires, often termed "happiness indexes"; 2) competency assessment measures, such as knowledge or skill tests (for example, multiple-choice examinations and performance on simulated clinical tests); 3) practice performance measures (such as test ordering and prescription writing); and 4) health care outcomes, such as blood pressures, pain scales, or patient satisfaction measures. See chapters 7 and 8 in *Leadership Careers in Medical Education*, another book in the *Teaching Medicine* series, for more information about programmatic and learner evaluation (34).

The Reality: Overcoming Barriers to Changing the CME Paradigm
Many barriers, of course, confront the idealized though more effective formats and construct of CME presented here. First, for most physicians, time

is a formidable barrier to an increased involvement in CME. This applies to the participants as well as the faculty. For the participants, CME, in its several-day, away-from-the-office mode, may be problematic. However, a more practice-embedded view of CME, in which team rounds, small-group case discussions, interactive problem-solving, and other sessions are part of the fabric of work—not a separate entity —will help to resolve this issue.

Second, physicians have been used to a model in which all clinical work contributes to their income; they may see CME as not contributing to—in fact, taking away from—remuneration. However, basing CME activities on reimbursable quality measures will ultimately shift the emphasis toward use of these measures as CME learning objectives. Finally, emphasis is moving away from hours-based CME participation toward credits for meaningful activity. This shift has occurred among the specialty boards, their counterpart specialty societies, the American Medical Association, and many other organizations. By using the strategies for overcoming barriers found in the preceding discussion on societal, government, and regulatory factors, the challenges to participation in the new CME can be overcome.

❖ Conclusion

This chapter has focused on a changing paradigm of CME, moving it from a teacher-centered model to one that pays close attention to learner-clinicians, their needs, and the needs of patients. As the new CME engages the teacher who is invested in this new model and are interested in improving clinical care and health care outcomes, so too does its application engage the internist-learner. This process is enabled by understanding the learner's practice setting, professional demands, and clinical concerns; developing and conducting a comprehensive, engaging educational activity to address perceived and unperceived needs; and assessing the effect of the activity across a continuum of outcomes.

REFERENCES

1. **Davis DA, Thomson MA, Oxman AD, Haynes RB.** Changing physician performance. A systematic review of the effect of continuing medical education strategies. JAMA. 1995;274:700-5.
2. **Bloom BS.** Effects of continuing medical education on improving physician clinical care and patient health: A review of systematic reviews. Int J Technol Assess Health Care. 2005;21:3:380-5.
3. **Thomson O'Brien MA, Freemantle N, Oxman AD, Wolf F, Davis DA, Herrin J.** Continuing education meetings and workshops: effects on professional practice and health care outcomes. Cochrane Database Syst Rev. 2001:CD003030.

4. **Marinopolous SS, Dorman T, Ratanawongsa N, Wilson LM, Ashar BH, Magaziner JL, et al.** Effectiveness of Continuing Medical Education. Bethesda, MD: Agency for Healthcare Research and Quality; 2007.

5. **Fox RD, Mazmanian PE, Putnam RW.** Changing and Learning in the Lives of Physicians. New York: Praeger; 1989.

6. **Davis DA, Barnes BE, Fox R.** The Continuing Professional Development of Physicians, From Research to Practice. Chicago: American Medical Assoc; 2003.

7. **Accreditation Council for Graduate Medical Education.** ACGME competencies: suggested best methods for evaluation. Accessed at www.acgme.org/Outcome/assess/tooltable.pdf.

8. **Knowles MS.** The Modern Practice of Adult Education: Andragogy Versus Pedagogy. New York: New York Assoc Pr; 1970.

9. **Sidorov J.** Retraining specialist physicians for primary care practice. Acad Med. 1997; 72:248-9.

10. **Brookfield SD.** Understanding and Facilitating Adult Learning: A Comprehensive Analysis of Principles and Effective Practices. San Francisco: Josey-Bass; 1986.

11. **Pathman DE, Konrad TR, Freed GL, Freeman VA, Koch GG.** The awareness-to-adherence model of the steps to clinical guideline compliance. The case of pediatric vaccine recommendations. Med Care. 1996;34:873-89.

12. **Ballard DJ.** Indicators to improve clinical quality across an integrated health care system. Int J Qual Health Care. 2003;15 Suppl 1:i13-23.

13. **Centers for Medicare & Medicaid Services.** Physician Quality Reporting Initiative (PQRI). Accessed at www.cms.hhs.gov/pqri.

14. **American Association of Medical Colleges.** New models for care delivery. Accessed at www.aamc.org/patientcare/newmodels.

15. **Federation of State Medical Boards.** Accessed at www.fsmb.org.

16. **Medical Board of California.** Accessed at www.medbd.ca.gov.

17. **Wasserman SI, Kimball HR, Duffy FD.** Recertification in internal medicine: a program of continuous professional development. Task Force on Recertification. Ann Intern Med. 2000;133:202-8.

18. **Duffy FD, Lynn LA, Didura H, Hess B, Caverzagie K, Grosso L, et al.** Self-assessment of practice performance: development of the ABIM Practice Improvement Module (PIM). J Contin Educ Health Prof. 2008;28:38-46.

19. **Accrediation Council for Continuing Medical Education.** Accessed at www.accme.org.

20. **Colliver JA.** Constructivism: the view of knowledge that ended philosophy or a theory of learning and instruction? Teach Learn Med. 2002;14:49-51.

21. **Ende J, ed.** Theory and Practice of Teaching Medicine. Philadelphia: ACP Pr; 2010.

22. **Wenger E.** Communities of practice and social learning systems. Organization. 2000;7: 225-246.

23. **Zwarenstein M, Reeves S, Barr H, Hammick M, Koppel I, Atkins J.** Interprofessional education: effects on professional practice and health care outcomes. Cochrane Database Syst Rev. 2001:CD002213.

24. **Guyatt GH, Sackett DL, Cook DJ.** Users' guides to the medical literature. II. How to use an article about therapy or prevention. B. What were the results and will they help me in caring for my patients? Evidence-Based Medicine Working Group. JAMA. 1994; 271:59-63.

25. **Straus S, Richardson S, Glasziou P.** Evidence Based Medicine. 3rd ed. London: Churchill Livingstone; 2005.

26. UptoDate. Accessed at www.utdol.com/online/login.do.

27. MDConsult. Acccessed at www.mdconsult.com.

28. Clin-eguide. Accessed at www.clineguide.com.

29. WebMD. Accessed at www.webmd.com.

30. **Dowie R.** A review of research in the United Kingdom to evaluate the implementation of clinical guidelines in general practice. Fam Pract. 1998;15:462-70.

31. **Davis D, Evans M, Jadad A, Perrier L, Rath D, Ryan D, et al.** The case for knowledge translation: shortening the journey from evidence to effect. BMJ. 2003;327:33-5.

32. **Dixon J.** Evaluation criteria in studies of continuing education in the health professions: a critical review and a suggested strategy. Eval Health Prof. 1978;1:47-65.

33. **Straus S, Haynes RB.** Managing evidence-based knowledge: the need for reliable, relevant and readable resources. CMAJ. 2009;180:942-945.

34. **Pangaro L, ed.** Leadership Careers in Medical Education. Philadelphia: ACP Pr; 2010.

Index